HAUNTED
SWANSEA
AND BEYOND

HAUNTED SWANSEA AND BEYOND

SOUTH WALES PARANORMAL RESEARCH

Dedication

South Wales Paranormal Research would like to dedicate *Haunted Swansea and Beyond* to baby Lolani, who was so eager to be a part of this project that she appeared two months early! Lolani is the first (though hopefully not the last) SWPR baby, and we all wish her health and happiness for the future.

Also we would like to mention Simon Hosier, who has still not left for Canada (for which we are very grateful!)

Frontispiece:
An atmospheric view of Pennard Castle.

First published 2008

The History Press
The Mill, Brimscombe Port
Stroud, Gloucestershire, GL5 2QG
www.thehistorypress.co.uk

Reprinted 2010, 2012, 2013

© South Wales Paranormal Research, 2008

The right of South Wales Paranormal Research to be identified as the Author of this work has been asserted in accordance with the Copyrights, Designs and Patents Act 1988.

All rights reserved. No part of this book may be reprinted or reproduced or utilised in any form or by any electronic, mechanical or other means, now known or hereafter invented, including photocopying and recording, or in any information storage or retrieval system, without the permission in writing from the Publishers.
British Library Cataloguing in Publication Data.
A catalogue record for this book is available from the British Library.

ISBN 978 0 7524 4457 4

Typesetting and origination by The History Press
Printed in Great Britain

Contents

Acknowledgements		6
Introduction		7
Chapter 1	Castle Ghosts	9
Chapter 2	Local Landmarks and their Fantastic Phantoms	27
Chapter 3	Hauntings in the Workplace	45
Chapter 4	Personal and Private Phenomena	59
Chapter 5	Spirits of the Great Outdoors	78

Acknowledgements

I would like to extend my deepest thanks to a great number of people who have contributed to the production of *Haunted Swansea and Beyond*, whether through their stories, pictures, interviewing of witnesses or editorial support. Without them, this book would not be in your hands now!

Some of those that have been kind enough to tell us of their experiences wish to remain anonymous, and some wish to be known only by their first name, so to the following people, and those not listed here (although you know who you are), I offer my gratitude for your willingness to share your tale!

Teresa John, Clare White, Mark Gulliford, Val Williams, Debra John, Brian Gent, Gareth Francis, Lesley Smith, Ashford Price, Lisa Williams, Tracey Ellis, Richard Rawlings, Krys Wareing, Brady Clarke, Heather and Gary Davies, Ainsley Page, Anthony Adams, Hywel and Beth, David Morgan, and Victoria Price (www.spooksparanormalinvestigators.co.uk).

In addition to these contributors I would like to offer particular thanks to a few individuals who have worked above and beyond the call of duty with this project. Firstly, to both Gareth Francis and Brian Gent who have been the providers of a great many of the stories in this book. Gareth has been a member of SWPR for a number of years now and has shown his commitment in many projects, and Brian is one of SWPR's newest members, joining us in early 2008, but has already shown us what an asset he is and will be for some time to come. An extra thanks to Richard Rawlings who gave his time to help us with a number of the pictures in the book from his hometown of Bridgend.

Also, to Graham White, who has spent many an evening tirelessly proofreading the text, and to my fiancée, Clare White, who has been the key figure in both pulling everything together ready to send to the publishers, and giving me a regular 'gentle' reminder of the deadline!

Once again SWPR has shown its enthusiasm and dedication towards their passion for sharing the paranormal heritage of Wales.

Thank you friends!

Steve Cluer
SWPR Chairman
July 2008

INTRODUCTION

www.SWPR.co.uk

As we quoted in the introduction to our first book, *Haunted Cardiff and the Valleys*, William Howells once said in his 1831 book *Cambrian Superstitions*,' ... more ghosts and goblins I think were prevalent in Wales, than in England or any other country'. At South Wales Paranormal Research, we firmly believe this claim, and in this book we would like to take you on a paranormal journey through some of the lesser-known stories from Swansea and beyond.

When it comes to areas of historic importance in the beautiful principality of Wales, few are as significant as Swansea and the surrounding valleys. Previously a prehistoric settlement dating back to 2,000 BC, it has now become the location of some of the world's most important prehistoric human remains. These remains were uncovered on the Gower Peninsula and have included the strange and mysterious 'Red Lady', a Neolithic-period skeleton discovered in Paviland Cave on the Gower's southern coast. In more recent years Swansea went on to be known as the birthplace of the world's first railway service. On 25 March 1807, a railroad carriage was converted to carry people. Its journey, from 'the dunes' in Swansea ending up at Mumbles, meant that its passengers became the first railway passengers in the world.

Swansea and its neighbouring counties have also been linked with some extremely important and wealthy families from Welsh history, and this is visible through many of the fantastic castles and buildings therein.

Through *Haunted Swansea and Beyond*, South Wales Paranormal Research would like to share with you a selection of tales of unexplained phenomena that have certainly taken our interest. Although there may be a few familiar and historical elements to the book, we have aimed to yet again bring you a compendium of stories 'straight from the horse's mouth', as they say. We have gathered these more recent experiences directly from witnesses in an attempt to ensure we have all the facts, untainted by word of mouth over time.

To be releasing this, our second book, just in time for South Wales Paranormal Research's fifth birthday is yet another achievement that we are very proud of. The group has grown and developed so much in the last five years, with new and enthusiastic members joining on a regular basis. We are all hopeful that the next five years will bring many more projects and surprises, and possibly another book to add to the series!

We sincerely hope that all of you enjoy your read, and are confident that there is something for everyone contained in the pages that follow. From tales of the paranormal in awe-inspiring castles along the Gower coast, to strange and wonderful phenomena in family homes in small villages further up the valley.

If any readers have stories of their own experiences from around Wales, we would love to hear from you and further develop our database of Welsh paranormal heritage.

Thank you for taking the time to read our book!
Diolch am fanteisio ar y cyfle i ddarllen ein llyfr!

One

Castle Ghosts

Wales as a principality boasts the largest collection of castles per square mile in the whole of Europe – a total of 641. From small Welsh-built strongholds to huge gothic-style mansions, it includes some of the most stunning buildings around, of which Swansea and its surrounding valleys certainly have their share. Many powerful families of the past have stamped their mark on the locality with their impressive architecture – names such as de Braose, le Bere, Rice Mansel and Talbots.

In this chapter, we visit the paranormal heritage of six of our favourites and would like to share the tales connected to them. We begin with Margam Castle, a site that holds a very special place in the heart of many SWPR members, and was voted last year as our most popular location visited.

Margam Castle, Port Talbot

Margam Castle is built on the site of an Iron Age settlement in Port Talbot, and the gothic structure was commissioned in 1830 by Christopher Rice Mansel Talbot. The building was once the site of another castle which was demolished to make way for an orange grove, and during the ten years it took to build, it is reported that there were several deaths attributed to masons falling whilst undertaking their work.

After completion, the castle then housed the Talbot family, who lived in this beautiful building with a small amount of house staff, gamekeepers and workmen. The family resided in the castle until the outbreak of the Second World War in 1939. Margam was then bought by David Evans Bevan, who found the upkeep of such a grand structure to be too much for him to carry on, and the castle was requisitioned by British and American forces for many different uses.

Margam Castle, c.1939.

After peace was announced, and the castle was no longer being used by the military, it fell into disrepair and was then purchased and lovingly restored by Glamorgan Council during the 1970s. Today, very few parts of the castle are accessible to the general public, unless conducting an overnight investigation, and the following are stories of experiences during two such nights – on the occasion of SWPR's Annual General Meeting, held at Margam Castle in 2008, and the first visit on 9 July 2005.

Going back to 2005 to begin with, the night was generally a very quiet one, with quite minimal activity to note. Despite the apparent lack of ghosts on a paranormal event, a great night was had by all, for the main reason that the building is just amazing and oozes with atmosphere. The following story is of a very unusual few minutes at around 5 a.m. spent by Steve and Gareth. To set the scene a little, just inside the huge doors of the castle is an extremely elaborate grand staircase rising into the upper floors. It is hard to explain just how magical this sight is and therefore we would just suggest you pay the castle a visit yourself, if only to see this staircase. At the bottom of the staircase against the wall was a very large and old wooden window frame, one with arc-shaped windows much as you would expect to find in a church. After descending the stairs from their last activity, both Steve and Gareth were drawn to the window frame and felt compelled to touch it and have a go at psychometry to see whether it held any past energy.

Upon touching the frame, both of them suddenly felt quite strange, and almost unwell. A feeling of quite overwhelming emotion had come over them leaving them feeling faint and hot. Steve then commented that he had the strangest image, of a young lady kneeling beside a river with her hands in the water, and a feeling of impending pain. Gareth then said that he

SWPR members at Margam Castle.

could sense the same thing, and felt that something was about to happen, that someone was about to join this young lady. Almost at the same time, both Steve and Gareth said that a man was quietly creeping up behind her with sinister intent.

By this time, the two men had been joined by another member of the group, who suggested that they say no more, but just try to finish the scene in their minds, and then write down independently what happened and any descriptions of the people involved. Thinking this would be an interesting experiment, they both agreed, and a few minutes later sat down and wrote down their information. Upon being read, it was clear that both had seen the same image of the man hitting the lady over the head with a long wooden stick, and she then fell into the water and drowned. Not only this, they both described the man in an almost identical way! Was this an example of psychometry at its best? Or was it a strange moment of one participant developing strange images and the other one being able to read his mind? We may never know, but either way it was a very strange and paranormal experience.

The second tale comes from the AGM on 5 April 2008. It had been a dreary and depressing week weather-wise, with rain and very cold temperatures for April. Gareth, Tracey, Lisa and Becky had arrived at the castle at approximately 2 p.m. so that Tracey and Gareth could assist the other members of the executive committee in preparing for the AGM and the overnight event. Everything during the afternoon ran as efficiently as expected, with very few problems. They had a meal in the café attached to the castle, and it was then on to the reason most people were there – spending a night in a very beautiful, historical building which was supposedly haunted. The weather was similar to the past week – extremely wet with constant rain, and even some light snow. The night was dark and foreboding.

The upper floor of Margam Castle.

Gareth was the lead investigator for Group 3 with other members Karen, Becky, Amanda, Geinor and fellow 'executive' Mark as the backmarker for the group. Throughout the night Mark had been audio recording every session, hopefully to pick up any EVP (electronic voice phenomena) that might have been present. It had been a pretty quiet night, with only a few unexplained occurrences. For example, at one point a few of the groups heard whistling at the same time (although in different locations throughout the castle) and had received some interesting information on the planchette, but otherwise generally pretty quiet.

It was at 2 a.m. that Gareth led his group into what is commonly known as the 'beam room' at the top of the castle for a glass-channelling experiment. They had been in the room for approximately thirty minutes, with some possibly interesting information being produced. At one point they believed they were in contact with a male member of the Air Force who was in the 562 Squadron, an officer nicknamed 'Legs'. They continued with their experiment, believing the spirit with whom they were communicating was a bit of a practical joker, with lots of contradictory replies.

Afterwards things began to take a very different form. They began to speak to a female spirit entity who stated that she was fifteen years old, and for some unknown reason Gareth then began asking questions in what little French he knew, to which the spirit replied it was easier if they spoke to her in English. This female spirit moved the glass to the letters MVMQM (which means very little, as even when using Roman numerals it does not really gave a date, with Q meaning nothing). She then moved to the letters MME (which is the French abbreviation of 'mademoiselle').

The glass that was being used was practically moving around the table by itself, and it then started to spell out the word Mielel, which Gareth stated that although spelt incorrectly, was very close to the French word for honey, 'miel'. It was at this point that chaos descended on the group. Karen, who was sitting to Gareth's left, mentioned the word Mia and then suddenly began to scream and tried to climb on top of him; Becky and Amanda also began to scream. It was only after a few minutes of reassurance that the entire group wanted to leave the room as soon as possible. At this point Steve and Neil came running through the open doorway to see if everyone was alright. From the other side of the building, outside in a garden area, they had heard the scream and came running, convinced that somebody was hurt, such was the level of fear in the voices they heard. Emotions were at an all-time high and a very perplexed and nervous group then walked back to the allocated 'base' room.

It was only then, in the safe and calm environment downstairs, that Karen explained what had happened to her. Whilst conducting the glass channelling, she felt that someone was looking over the empty chair next to her, and that then a figure had suddenly pounced towards her, which had resulted in her screaming. It was after this that Mark realised that the session had been recorded on his voice recorder, and this was when the next strange moment took place. On the tape, just before Karen started screaming, was a ghostly and unknown whisper repeating the name 'Mia'. Gareth felt positive that he could rule out all the other members in the group as he knew their voices well and they just did not fit! When conducting a feedback session at the end of the event, the night guard who was working on duty stated that the name Mia had only been brought up once before and that it was related somehow to the castle, and that they would have to access the castle archives to find out more. Something which they fully intend to follow up.

Pennard Castle, Three Cliffs Bay

Perched on the high ground overlooking the beautiful Three Cliffs Bay and Pennard Pill on the Gower Peninsular are the ruins of the thirteenth-century castle of Pennard. Situated on the very edge of a golf course it is a pleasant walk from the nearest road as several public footpaths easily access it. The views through the north curtain-wall gateway are spectacular and have found a place into many photo albums. Its builders were not the finest around at the time and, coupled with the sandy nature of its surroundings, it soon sounded the death knell for the castle. As it was already a ruin by late medieval times, its reputation began to be surrounded by myth and legend and this was soon to be interwoven into the supernatural framework of Wales. The castle has therefore gained the reputation of being the ruin with the longest history of haunting in the principality. Due to its elevated position and placement on open ground, it is easily observed from the campsite across the pill at North Hills Farm and the chalets at the Sandy Lane complex.

The first specific event happened to a group of college students who were spending a long weekend in the 1970s under the stars on several south Gower beaches. It was a fine weekend, so armed with sleeping bags they settled around a campfire and after an evening of music and talking they all drifted off to sleep. Several of them were awoken in the early hours by what sounded like a woman's scream coming from the direction of the castle above them.

A view of Three Cliffs Bay, taken from Pennard Castle.

At first they thought it was an owl or seabird but when all of them, now fully awake, heard the cry again they decided to send two of their number up to investigate. The two men chosen ascended the path up to the castle, with the bright moonlight giving the castle silhouette ahead an eerie glow. Suddenly one of them stopped as he felt a distinct cold breeze on his left side, which he later described as if something invisible was passing him at close quarters. They both searched the castle and its surroundings but there were no obvious signs of the source of the mysterious sound. They returned back down to the group to report on their findings, only to find two more of their fellow students making their way up towards them. It transpired that when the two of them had been highlighted by the moonlight, some dark shapes had been moving along the wall and then appeared to descend the path on a collision course with the ascending pair. They monitored the path and castle over the next hour without any further incident and then returned to their temporary campsite.

The next day, still worried by their experience, they asked the local shopkeeper in the village if he knew of anything that could be causing the effects. A local villager, in the shop at the time, claimed that such noises were sometimes heard and had been put down to the wind movement through architectural features of the castle. The students were not convinced and went on their way convinced that they had just experienced a paranormal event. It was just as well these students were not aware of the stories. A woman's ghost is claimed to haunt the castle with a piercing scream that is said to send mad anyone who spends too long there at night. This may come from the folk tale that a woman allegedly threw herself to her death in the river below after her lover had been killed. However, this tale may alternatively originate from the 'Gwrach-y-rhibyn' legend, regarding a spectral creature similar to the Irish 'banshee', whose

Pennard Castle.

screeching voice was believed to be a harbinger of death. This particular legend is to be heard in many parts of the principality.

By far the most reported phenomena at Pennard Castle are the strange coloured lights seen dancing around the ruined walls. These are known as the fairy or ghost lights. The first documented sighting is believed to have been in the nineteenth century, so this rules out any effects from modern technology. Visitors to the area have reported most of the sightings in recent years, as the locals appear to be reticent to discuss the matter. Perhaps this is because there is a local tradition passed down through the generations that the place has been cursed on more than one occasion. Folklore tells that an old Welsh magician, versed in the ancient ways, built the castle in one day and night and somehow invoked the wrath of a fellow magician who cast a spell on it, causing it to fall down. This theme of the two magicians fighting is common throughout British and European folklore, although a much more relevant tale exists that may explain why they are still called the fairy lights and also show that this phenomena has been around for a considerable time.

The events that led to the second curse were said to have started with the return to Pennard Castle of a noted Welsh chieftain. The story goes that amongst his spoils of a recent battle, he had gained the hand of the daughter of the ruler of all Wales. Naturally, a great feast was prepared on his return to celebrate his victory and prize. The celebration banquet was in full swing when the outer guard raised the alarm that they were being attacked. Rushing to their defences, the soldiers reported seeing the lights of what they took to be a raiding party on the beach of Three Cliffs Bay. The chief assessed the situation and decided to deal with the advancing enemy himself, as by their size they posed little threat. Grabbing his sword and ordering his men to follow, the chief raced down the hill from the castle to engage the raiding party who had dared disturb his victory celebrations. When he arrived on the beach he rubbed his eyes in disbelief, as facing him were a troop of fairy folk dancing around coloured globes of light. Fearful of their kind the chief ordered them slain and his men immediately charged in with swords slashing left and right. What he did not know was that these ethereal beings were immune to harm from humans and just became angry at his actions. The leader of the fairies put a curse on the chief and his castle that has remained to this day. The fairy leader also claimed that the ruler's daughter would become his wife but never bear any children; this also allegedly came true.

Similar mysterious lights have been reported all over the world; they are most commonly described as being white, blue, green or yellow, and predominately spherical in shape. Since ancient times such lights have been associated with the souls of the dead. They have also gained the name of 'Ignis Fatuus', which is Latin for 'foolish fire' – this is probably because it is seen as foolhardy to try and capture or even get close to them. In Germany they are said to follow funeral processions, whereas in the Scandinavian countries such lights are believed to be the spirits of unbaptised babies. In England they are known 'Will-o-the-wisp' or 'Jack o' Lantern', thought by some to be a bad omen. Scottish people call it the 'corpse light' or 'corpse candle', and in South America they are just referred to as the 'evil lights'. Sceptics offer a range of other causes for these phenomena such as electricity, magnetism, swamp gas or natural phosphorescence.

Pennard Castle is a good example of how we have, down the ages, explained unknown phenomena with a cocktail of mythology, legend and actual history. It also portrays how an historic castle, whose origins we know little about, can spawn such tales.

Twin Castles of Ogmore, Bridgend

Close to where the Ogmore River flows into the Bristol Channel, and near to its confluence with the Ewenny River, it is guarded on either side by two castles. Many will be familiar with Ogmore Castle and its picturesque location by the river with the adjacent ford and stepping stones. However, on the opposite side of the river, hidden in the trees, are the much more atmospheric ruins of Candleston Castle. It is not a true castle but actually a fortified manor house dating back to the fourteenth century. It was altered many times and eventually abandoned some time in the nineteenth century. The name Candleston may have been derived from the name Cantilupe, as this property and its surrounding lands are believed to have belonged to this Welsh family of Norman ancestry. These days it is a rapidly deteriorating ivy-covered ruin that was once the centre point of the lost village of Treganlaw and its surrounding farmlands.

There is much folklore surrounding Candleston, and even in these modern times it is said to be a very paranormally active location. The ancient village of Treganlaw and most of the seaward side of the castle and estate now lies under the mighty sand dunes of Merthyr Mawr Warren. A recent theory is that the village was lost during the flood of 1607, and this is when the sand was first deposited as a result of this catastrophe. The ruin has a reputation of being very active supernaturally, and anyone who goes there is immediately aware of the dark, dank and eerie atmosphere. Many old stones and crosses are to be found around Candleston, most of them coming from a much earlier period of our history. There is one area in particular where dark shadows are seen to this day around a stone, provocatively named in the past as 'The Goblin Stone'. Once the sun has gone down people visiting this area are apparently inexplicably drawn to this stone and feel the urge to put their arms around it. Once they have embraced the stone they find it increasingly difficult to let go. A few years ago a psychic went through this process and actually visualised creepers weaving an invisible net around him and the stone. He also reported seeing many hands coming out of the ground. It is interesting to note that the Welsh name for the nearby lost village can be translated as 'The town of a hundred hands'.

Another spectre seen regularly throughout the whole area is a white lady. She has been seen in both Ogmore Castle, Candleston, and also in the grounds of nearby Ewenny Priory. A few years ago one eyewitness almost crashed his car as the spectre glided across the B4524 near Ogmore Castle. Perhaps the lady used to make the journey between the three sites? With a safe crossing place at the ancient stepping stones, the route between the three sites is almost direct and may have even older origins. The stones at Candleston are believed to have come from an early Christian Celtic church on the site, and the route between this and another early ecclesiastical site at Ewenny Priory may be a so-called 'Death Road' or 'Spirit Path'. Such ways were used in ancient times as ritual routes to carry bodies of the important deceased to any special burial ground. Even after this use had been abandoned the reputation of these ways lived on in local folklore as the haunts of ghosts and fairy folk. Whatever the explanation, it is obvious that this spectre has been around for a long time, as in Ewenny there are places called White Lady's Meadow and a road named White Lady's Lane. However, the spectral lady is not the only apparition to use this river crossing.

The stepping stones leading from Ogmore Castle towards Candleston Castle.

Ogmore Castle.

There have been many reports of a ghostly coach or cart drawn by four horses rapidly moving to the centre of the ford by Ogmore Castle, at which point it disappears. Many have seen this apparition down the years and have related it to a tragic incident that once happened there. In those days there were no bridges over either of the rivers and they had to be crossed at shallow points by fords. The Ewenny River's ford was, as it is today, close to the castle, whereas the Ogmore was crossed at a ford near where Merthyr Mawr village is today. It is said that although it was a fine evening there, a deluge was coming down in the upper valleys. The coachman or waggoner is believed not to have noticed the sudden rise in water level and plunged into the unseen raging torrent. The coach or cart was washed away to sea and never seen again. However, the most interesting tale from this general area is yet to come.

Like the White Lady, there have been many sightings and sounds of strange dogs over the years in this area. Candleston has been used in the recent past as a film location, and although it is the ideal location for a horror movie it was the crew of another famous film that experienced the next activity. Believe it or not, some scenes from *Lawrence of Arabia* were filmed on the sand dunes. Technicians and security were working late one night in their temporary compound on the edge of the wood close to the castle, when they heard what they took to be a dog howling close by. Thinking it was the security guard dog, at first they took no notice, and then the security man emerged from his caravan without his dog. He claimed that it was not his Alsatian guard dog, and in fact his dog was refusing to come out. They then saw a low shadowy shape in the trees that could have been a big dog, but none of them were brave enough to investigate.

Black Dog folklore is pretty widespread in South Wales so these tales are not surprising. However, it was not until research was undertaken into the family that built and owned

Candleston that some curious facts came to light. Cantilupe in old Latin can be interpreted as a 'running wolf', and the family crest is said to have been a wolf's head, holding in its mouth a broken spear with five drops of blood. In ancient times wolves were hunted in Wales to exterminate them and no doubt some brave act of saving a life from a wolf's clutches may have given rise to this family's heraldic design. What is more interesting is that the Cantilupes were related to the Baskerville family who shared the same heraldic device. Do you think then that Sir Arthur Conan Doyle knew about these families when he created his fictional hound of death?

Oystermouth Castle, Mumbles

On the banks of the famous Mumbles in Swansea stands the majestic Oystermouth Castle, with its fantastic views over Swansea Bay. The castle was constructed by William de Londres in the early twelfth century, and was burned down on two occasions by the Welsh, the first in 1116 and the second in 1215.

In the thirteenth century the Lords of Gower – the de Braose's – held the castle, and with their standing moved the focus of principal residency from Swansea to Oystermouth. The lords slowly rebuilt the castle out of stone, and it is the work from this time period which remains to this day.

The castle stands on what is now commonly known as Newton Road, and is fairly well preserved from the days when it was in the control of the de Braoses. You may be thinking that with all the history and destruction that revolves around the castle it must be home to a plethora of ghosts. However, this is not the case. Apparently very little paranormal activity takes place here, except for one strange event which keeps repeating itself and refuses to die away. This is Peter's story.

It was a normal wet night in Mumbles in March 2003. Peter was driving himself home from Swansea back to Mumbles, after having been to the cinema with his girlfriend. After dropping her home, he paid very close attention to the road and the cars in front due to the bad weather. It was surprisingly busy for 10 p.m. on a Wednesday night, and Peter deduced that there were probably many couples who had decided to go for a romantic stroll along the waterfront, and were now making a mad dash for their warm dry homes.

Peter was getting closer to home and the traffic which had been slowing him down had now finally veered off in other directions. He was close to Oystermouth Castle, when he suddenly saw a movement on the battlements. On closer inspection he was sure that he could see a young woman. She appeared to be in distress and Peter, being a kind and conscientious person, pulled the car over to see if he could be of any assistance.

As he turned to walk up the slope towards the castle the figure turned. Peter was shocked to find that the back of the woman's dress had been torn away, and bloody welts could be seen covering her skin. Thinking that she had been mugged, or worse, he hurriedly made his way to the castle gates. On arrival he could clearly see the place in which she was standing. She was in pain, sobbing bitterly, and as he tried to enter the castle he discovered that the gates were locked shut. He tried in vain to climb the gates to access the castle, but could not get in. He called to the girl, who either could not hear him or refused to reply to his shouts.

Oystermouth Castle pre-1950.

Oystermouth Castle as it is today.

Whilst calling out for the fifth time and beckoning for the woman to make her way towards him, Peter suddenly realised that she had vanished. Thinking the worst, that she might have thrown herself or fallen over the battlements, he quickly made his way around the castle to her last position. Fortunately he found no one, but where she had vanished to became even more of a mystery. He searched and searched the surrounding area, but found nothing. The woman had completely disappeared.

On researching who or what this ghostly apparition could be, the only information that could be found are stories of a woman who is believed to have been flogged to death on a whipping post, some of which still stand in the castle's dungeons to this day. But who she was or what she had done to warrant such a severe punishment will forever remain a mystery.

Craig y Nos Castle, Pen-y-cae

Back in early September 2004, Clare was asked by her friend Bonita to help in her charity Spookathon that she had organised for her workmates. Taking place in Craig y Nos Castle, a rather strange location, she jumped at the chance. Built in 1843, Craig y Nos is a mysterious rambling castle which has grown and expanded throughout the years. With a past consisting of opera singers and theatre, combined with its use as a tuberculosis (TB) hospital during the early 1900s, it has certainly seen its fair share of visitors – some closer to death than others.

With all the participants of the Spookathon gathered safely in the 'Nurse's Block' – now a collection of simple bedrooms housed within the previous accommodation block for the nurses who treated the dying TB patients – the night was about to start. The black clouds that had hovered threateningly for most of the day had just started to release their first drops of rain, and the breeze was growing gradually into a substantial wind – the perfect atmosphere for a spooky night in an even spookier castle. The group was split into three teams, and each team was allocated to a team leader, Bonita being one of them and Clare another. Three areas of the castle were to be investigated – the theatre, the bedrooms and the area Clare's group were to start in, the cellars.

Her group made their way to the dark, silent cellars. As they descended the steep steps a sense of apprehension was clear within the group. Staying huddled together, the group took a good look around the area, jumping now and again at a small noise or two, often resulting from another member of the group. By the time their session in the cellars had come to an end, everyone was feeling much more relaxed. By no means was anybody happy, standing in the depths of Craig y Nos' darkest areas, but very little had happened to warrant anyone feeling overly scared.

After a rush through the constant drizzle and heightening wind back to the Nurse's Block for a quick hot drink and biscuits, the groups were ready to depart again. This time Clare's group was heading to the theatre. Craig y Nos Castle and grounds were once the estate of the celebrated opera diva, Adelina Patti, who during her lifetime (1843-1919) became one of the world's most famous and highly rewarded entertainers. The beautiful Victorian theatre was installed especially for Madame Patti, and there are rumours that even now she can be heard singing within its walls.

An old postcard of Craig y Nos Castle.

At the far end of the theatre, opposite the stage, are a set of large patio doors. It was through these that Clare and her group gained welcome shelter from the worsening weather outside in the relative comfort of the theatre. Feeling more confident after surviving the dark cellars, the group took seats on the stage surrounding a table. As the wind howled outside, the group closed their eyes, joined hands and Clare asked gently, 'If there's anyone here with us, if Madame Patti is with us now, please make yourself known …'

Suddenly, the double doors at the far end of the theatre swung outwards with a crash, and the wind howled in to the auditorium. Without saying a word everyone in the group jumped up from their seats, and after a brief pause started to giggle! So who was to blame for not shutting the door properly? No one could remember who was last to enter the theatre, but with that wind blowing a gale outside, the doors must have opened due to that. Mustn't they? Clare climbed down from the stage and rushed to the back of the theatre to close the doors before too much rain got in, ensuring they were securely closed this time. The rest of the session passed pretty quietly, the doors stayed firmly shut, and they were soon heading back for a warming cup of tea before the next session.

The next area for Clare's group was the deserted bedrooms area. This part of the castle was rarely used and had not yet been restored. One of the rooms is specifically called Patti's Bedroom, believed to be the actual bedroom of Adelina Patti during her ownership of the house. Bonita's group had just been in that area, and they had set up a digital voice recorder in that bedroom, leaving it to record. Armed with this information, a now quite cheerful group followed Clare into the main body of the castle. Through a noisy door that slammed behind them, and up a flight of wooden steps, they walked into the dingy corridor of the first floor,

Craig y Nos Castle, showing the patio doors that lead into the theatre.

their footsteps echoing on the wooden floors. In this area they could clearly see the poor state of disrepair the castle had reached during the latter half of the 1900s. The group, while still quite buoyant, fell silent as they started to explore the area. They found Madame Patti's bedroom – a rather empty shell with nothing to speak of other than a few random plastic chairs, a carpet, beautiful full-wall windows, which in the daytime would be looking over the gorgeous local landscape, and Bonita's digital voice recorder in the centre of the floor. Making sure their arrival was voiced clearly into the recorder, including the time and members' names, the group stood in a circle in the centre of the room, linked hands, and once again started calling out. After some time, and a lack of response from anything 'otherworldly', they dropped their hands only to hear one of the most frightening sounds they had heard all night. A high female scream echoed up the stairs into the bedroom, causing half the group to rush to the doorway.

'Wait!' shouted Clare. As the group stopped and stood still, hearts pounding, hearing nothing but their own breathing and the blood rushing through their adrenaline-filled bodies, another noise echoed up through the building. The sound of giggling, followed by another scream and more giggling. It was soon clear that Bonita's group, who were now in the cellars, had obviously wound themselves up quite a bit and had started jumping – and screaming – at their own shadows. The cellars, although two floors down, were almost directly below where Clare's group currently stood, and the noise was filtering through quite clearly.

After some nervous laughter, and a quick explanation to the still-recording digital voice recorder, the group discussed what to do next. The consensus was to continue through this floor to the rooms at the end of the corridor. As they made their way down the corridor, heading into areas yet undiscovered, torches shining through the gloom, they all suddenly heard another unexpected noise – the door at the bottom of the staircase slam closed, and the hurried footsteps of someone coming up the stairs. Judging from the earlier hysterics, they guessed it was probably a member of Bonita's group, either rushing up to explain what the screams were all about, or maybe to try to play a trick on them. Mischievously the group made a quick decision to play a trick on whoever it was that was heading up the stairs towards them. They rushed to the end of the corridor and into the room right at the end, each member finding somewhere to hide – behind the door, in a dark alcove, behind a piece of furniture. Stifling giggles, they hid and tried to stay as still as possible, waiting. And they waited. Until they realised that the footsteps that had been heading up the stairs never made it to the top. No footsteps were heard on the wooden floor of the corridor, and no footsteps were heard descending the stairs again … so where did they go? Whispering to each other, Clare's group trod quietly back out into the corridor and started looking around to try to see where this person could have gone. On inspection, without making any further noise, the owner of the footsteps could only have vanished. As a shiver ran up the spines of each member of the group, they were glad to see that time had beaten them and it was time to return to the cosy glow of the Nurse's Block.

As soon as Bonita's group joined Clare's group in the Nurse's Block, accusations flew. Had they been screaming? Yes, they had! As suspected! Who was it who came upstairs? No one, the group had stayed together the whole time. On asking both the third group and the member of staff, who was on site for safety, whether any of them had come upstairs, they had still not reached a conclusion. So who was it who had rushed upstairs? And where did they go?

About a month later, Clare was visiting Bonita, and the conversation turned to the night at Craig y Nos Castle. Bonita suddenly remembered that the digital voice recorder she had left running all night had never been listened to. Perfect, thought Clare, the footsteps will be on there.

Bonita rushed off to fetch the voice recorder, and they sat in the quiet house listening to the tape. There was Bonita, setting up the recording. Bonita's group calling out, and then leaving. Then a gap of perfect silence. Soon there was the sound of many footsteps and Clare's group arriving, doing their calling out, and even the sound of a distant scream, followed by an explanation to the tape. Clare's group leaving and then nothing. Where were the footsteps? They re-wound the recording and listened again, but no, the footsteps definitely were not there. They left the recording playing as they discussed this strange phenomena. By now, the recording was replaying the silence during the time the groups were all safely in the warmth of the Nurse's Block. As they paused in their conversation, listening to the silent whirring of the recording, from the machine there came a very definite and very female sigh.

Almost a year later, two friends, Lisa and Geinor, were delighted to be presented with their birthday presents from their partners – they were to spend the night on a paranormal investigation at the castle, before retiring to one of the en-suite bedrooms.

The two friends were excited at the prospect of spending the night at Craig y Nos, but nervous after having watched a television programme about the apparent phenomena there. On arrival, they were perturbed to discover that they had been allocated the same haunted bedroom where the television presenter had slept and had experienced strange occurrences! The friends were not to return to this room until 4 a.m.

There were quite a few highlights during their night at Craig y Nos. While in Madame Patti's Boudoir, on the floor where the children's ward was situated, children's footsteps and voices

The lovingly restored fountain outside Craig y Nos Castle.

could be clearly heard by all in the group. Lisa says, 'This was very spooky, although very sad too.' Allegedly people have witnessed apparitions of children's spirits on various occasions there. However, it all went quiet when the two friends and their group ascended to investigate the top floor. The morgue in the cellar, where Madame Patti's body was kept before being buried in Paris, was also particularly eerie with strange tapping sounds heard and cold spots felt by all.

In the early hours of the morning, Lisa and Geinor returned to their bedroom, where they went on to experience some further unusual phenomena. They sat together and asked if there were any spirits present; if so, to give them a sign. The two ladies simultaneously felt pain in their heads almost as if there was some sort of vice or grip putting pressure on their skulls. Only recently while researching old photos of TB patients at the castle, Lisa came across some pictures of children wearing unusual headgear – maybe for protective or medical purposes. Could they be linked? Were Lisa and Geinor picking up the feelings and emotions of previous residents of the castle? It certainly seems as though Craig y Nos is home to some very unusual phenomena and many strong feelings.

Two

Local Landmarks and their Fantastic Phantoms

Local landmarks, and buildings of significant historical and cultural importance, are in abundance all over the principality, and Swansea and its neighbours have a collection of their own to be extremely proud of. Many of these places are visited on a daily basis by hundreds of visitors, both locals and tourists alike, and have large and busy staff teams working within them. When you consider the history with which some of these sites are linked, it is hardly any wonder that tales of strange experiences and hauntings are being told all around.

In this chapter we have gathered a selection of stories from some of the most visited attractions in Wales, and we begin with one of our favourites, Dan-yr-Ogof Caves. This hugely impressive cave system is one of the premier days out in Wales, and SWPR has spent many an hour investigating its reputed ghosts.

Dan-yr-Ogof Showcaves, Abercrave

On Friday 18 August 2006 a team of nine SWPR-trained investigators met at 9 a.m. at Dan-Yr-Ogof Showcaves. They were starting a twenty-four-hour sit-in at Dan-Yr-Ogof as a way to kick off a six-week investigation into the paranormal activity in the caves. The sit-in was to raise money for the charity they support, the Cystic Fibrosis Trust. The caves can be found on the A4076, the road between Brecon and Swansea in South Wales.

The caves were discovered by two local brothers called Tommy and Jeff Morgan. Back in 1912 they travelled quite a distance into the cave system, even crossing an underground lake by using a one-man fishing boat called a coracle. They found their way by candlelight, and marked arrows in the sand on the floors so they did not get lost. But their adventure came to an end as they came up against a very tight passageway which they were unable to crawl

The entrance to Dan-yr-Ogof Showcaves.

through. That passage was later explored in 1963 by a member of the South Wales Caving Club, a local lady called Eileen Davis, but modern-day cavers say there is still a vast area yet to be discovered.

That Friday morning the members of SWPR met outside the entrance of the caves. They set up boards with information about the group, what they were doing there and the charity for which they were raising money. The owner of the caves, Ashford Price, met them and they discussed the day and night ahead of them.

Throughout the day they took it in turns either to stay at the entrance to the caves or to spend time in the furthest area, called the Bridge, which is near an indoor waterfall system. Those in the caves spent their time taking readings of temperature, humidity and wind speed, whilst talking to visitors. Those at the cave entrance also spoke to visitors explaining who they were and why they were there, and told them to look out for the investigators inside the caves.

Once the caves had closed to the public for the day, the intrepid members of SWPR then gathered together their equipment, food and drink, sleeping bags and other bits and pieces needed for the long, dark, cold and damp night ahead of them.

Ashford, the owner, saw them into the caves, gave plenty of warnings and advice concerning hypothermia (thank goodness they had a first-aider to hand!) and caves flooding, wished the team 'good luck', and then locked the outer door of the cave system. They then took the long 500-metre walk into the caves.

They had decided on two areas to stay during the night: the Cauldron chamber and the Bridge area, as these were the largest areas in the cave system, giving them plenty of room to set up their chairs, camp beds and sleeping bags. However, they soon realised that due to the constant drips of water falling from the cave's ceiling it was going to be very difficult to keep anything dry.

Everyone then sat down, chatted, and played games like 'I-spy'. Yes, 'I-spy' in the caves – that game soon ran out of ideas! After a while they decided to have a walk around the caves, partially to keep their circulation going, but also to see if they could witness any of the paranormal experiences that many of the staff had reported during their working day. The investigators took readings with their scientific equipment throughout, hoping to find some explanation. After a while, they all headed back to the Cauldron area with nothing to report.

Later in the night three male investigators, Mark, Richard and Andrew, decided to have a walk around to see if anything would happen to a smaller group. They headed off with a camcorder and camera hoping to see some phenomena, leaving the remaining six chatting quietly to each other in the Cauldron Cave.

After a ten-minute walk the intrepid three came to the area know as 'The Nuns' and 'The Angel'. These were names given to the stalactite and stalagmite formations which resemble an angel and a group of nuns. From this part of the caves they could not hear the rest of the group at all. They stayed in that area for between ten and fifteen minutes, filming and taking pictures before heading off around the rest of the cave system. After being absent from the group for thirty minutes, they returned thinking they had nothing to show for their efforts.

The group had a final chat about the night so far and then decided to try to get some rest, so they headed off to their sleeping bags. This was not an easy task, as once the torches were out the darkness was total. Mark had never seen darkness like that before – he could not even see his hand in front of his face. The constant water dripping on to them and the very cold temperature did not help much either, but Mark insists that was part of the fun of it.

Mark could not get to sleep so he decided just to sit there and keep an eye out in case something or someone made an unexpected visit. Mark was just thinking that the night was passing very slowly when something happened to get his adrenalin going. Towards the entrance to the Cauldron chamber, which leads to the tunnels heading towards the entrance to the cave system, Mark saw a male figure standing on the steps, staring at him. He waved at the figure. He said, 'I don't know why I waved at him, it seemed a good idea at the time, just to try to get some reaction from him.' Mark has described the figure as 'a male in his mid thirties, black hair with a brown flat cap on, black moustache, a brown kind of suit on, dating from around the early twentieth century. He just stood there staring at me as I waved, then he just disappeared.' Could he have been one of the Morgan brothers taking a walk through their caves making sure

Deep inside the Dan-yr-Ogof cave system.

everything was okay? It could not have been one of the staff members playing a joke as Mark had put a number of hidden motion sensors out in the corridor, so that if someone had been thinking of playing a joke, the alarms would have gone off to warn them that someone was about. But none of the alarms had sounded.

Mark wasn't the only one to see something strange during the night. Andrew woke up at one point, sat up in his reclining garden chair, and was convinced that he saw water rising up around him. Steve, another of the team members, woke to see what he could only describe as a 'Gollum-like creature' crawling up his camp bed. However, feeling so tired, Steve decided that he 'couldn't be bothered with it' so just turned over and went back to sleep! Of course, both these accounts were due to over-active imaginations and dreams … or were they?

At 9.30 a.m. on Saturday morning, Ashford unlocked the outside door and went to greet the investigators to see how they had fared during the night. They told him of their experiences, then packed up and headed off home for some proper rest.

Later that day, Mark watched back his camcorder tape. It seemed that the night had been more eventful than he had realised. He appeared to have captured some EVP (electronic voice phenomena). EVP is the recording of a voice on tape which is not heard at the time of recording, and it is believed that these voices are from ghosts or spirits.

Whilst at the Nuns and Angel formations with his two colleagues, one of them asked, 'Where are we?' On the tape this is heard very clearly, but then, to Mark's surprise, a female voice whispered 'Angel' in response. The voice was very clear, and seemed to be up close to the camcorder. At the time of the recording all the female members were at least a ten-minute walk away from the three men, so Mark knew it could not have been any of them speaking.

'The Angel' formation, in Dan-yr-Ogof Showcaves.

Then again, on the tape, in the same area of the caves, Mark heard another female voice, this time seemingly talking in French. Mark asked a friend's daughter, who speaks French, to translate it. The translation seemed to be, 'I don't like it'. What don't they like? And why speak in French in a cave system in the heart of the Welsh valleys?

Actually, the French theme fits very nicely with Dan-yr-Ogof. There is evidence that the Morgan brothers bought a water-powered turbine from France; perhaps some French workers came over with the turbine to help them fit it and maybe, if they brought their families, one of their wives, sisters or daughters visited the caves and did not like some thing there.

Who knows the reasons behind it, but SWPR still have the evidence on tape.

This was not the last activity experienced by SWPR in Dan-yr-Ogof. As mentioned at the beginning of this story, this twenty-four-hour event was to kick-start a six-week investigation. This investigation was conducted every Friday night for the next six weeks, and proved to be just as interesting as the first night. Throughout the period, many investigators heard strange sounds from parts of the cave system they had not yet reached, often sounds of singing voices or children's laughter, but it was a night of strange psychic experiences that are worthy of further mention.

On the first of the six investigations, Steve, Neil and a female investigator we will name Katie, were teamed up and started their night sitting at a junction where the caves split into two directions to create a loop further in. As they were sitting there quietly, Katie, who was currently training to develop her own psychic skills, turned to Steve and said that she could see a man standing behind him. She went on to describe a man whose description perfectly fitted an uncle that had passed some years back, but that she could have known nothing about. She continued to talk about personality traits, hobbies and interests, all with surprising accuracy. To end this session, Katie asked the spirit to give them a sign that he could hear them, at which precise point a generator on the wall nearby suddenly kicked into action for a few seconds.

As if this single experience wasn't unusual enough, about an hour later when sitting by the Bridge chamber, Steve, who has not undertaken any psychic training, suddenly had some very strong images. These images he recounted, and he described the layout of a house, its garden, many of the ornaments and pieces of furniture including their locations, upholstery and even some personality traits he felt were associated with the house's owner. Little did he know that he was describing Katie's grandmother's home to a tee, right down to the smallest detail. How he suddenly developed this ability is still unknown, and it is not a skill he has been able to repeat, but it does raise the question of whether perhaps some certain locations are able to act as a conduit for psychic abilities and experiences.

Dan-yr-Ogof is certainly a very unusual and atmospheric location, and one the team would love to visit again sometime.

Rhossili Rectory, Rhossili

Located seven miles from Swansea, the Gower Peninsular boasts many strange and wonderful pieces of history occurring throughout the area: sunken ships, Arthur's Stone, The Giants Grave (a burial chamber dating back to approximately 3,500 BC) and Pennard Castle to name but a few. The peninsula is also scattered with caves, which supposedly held the oldest human and animal remains dating back to the Stone Age.

An old postcard of Rhossili Bay, including the Rhossili Rectory.

The majestic Worm's Head, overlooked by the Rhossili Rectory.

Rhossili Rectory.

Situated on the Gower Peninsula stands Rhosilli Rectory, which is tucked away in a very lonely spot between the cliffs. It is halfway between Llangennith and Rhosilli, and is where the original rector was supposed to have administered both churches. The rectory was once part of an ancient village, deserted around the fourteenth century. By the mid-eighteenth century it had fallen into disrepair, but was lovingly restored in the 1850s and then later bought by the National Trust in 1995.

The rectory is surrounded by beautiful scenery, and it is impossible to believe anything spooky or frightening could possibly happen here, but on more than one occasion something has. There are tales of ghostly sightings both in the rectory itself and along the beach by which it sits. Our story here recounts the experience of a young man and occurred in recent years. David was working with a paranormal group in early November 2002. He had worked with the group many times before, and found them to be honest people who really enjoyed their work.

It had been a fairly normal Saturday, and the weather for that day meant that it was raining but that there was very little wind. David had gone to bed early on the Friday in preparation for the long day ahead, and when Saturday came he and a few friends had met up and had a lovely meal in one of the many restaurants on the Mumbles. As David is a recovering alcoholic who has been 'dry' for three years he did not partake of any alcohol, and his friends had only a glass of wine each. It was then time to go back to the car and head for the rectory.

It was a fairly uneventful evening in the building with very few paranormal occurrences, except the usual small bangs and creaks being heard. But these could not be classed as paranormal for certain, as none of them had been there before, so it could have been merely the floors settling. There were a few cold spots which were not so easy to explain, and these were dotted around the entire location, but could not be confirmed as being spirit entities.

It was approximately 2 a.m. when David and his friend were in the hallway. His friend, who had been feeling unwell, had had to disappear to the bathroom, leaving him alone briefly. David was not scared or uneasy at being left alone in a supposedly haunted location – he had his torch for light and a radio in case he needed assistance. After a few minutes of walking around, he decided to find somewhere to sit down, and it was a few moments later when he heard the door opening at the other end of the hallway, followed by a sudden blast of cold air. Thinking it was just his friend who had finished in the bathroom, David didn't bother to turn around but just sat there waiting patiently.

It was then that he got the fright of his life, because whilst sitting there he heard a whispered voice say something along the lines of 'Why don't you turn and face me?', and, needless to say, this was not the voice of his friend. By David's own admission he ran through the building to the other exit and out of the rectory at a rate of knots! He has vowed that he will never step foot in Rhosilli Rectory again, either during the day or night, and has decided to assist no longer in paranormal investigations.

Who could it have been that wanted David to 'Turn and face' him? We may never know the answer for sure, but we can possibly link it to a couple of old tales connected with the rectory. One ex-vicar of the parish who lived in the rectory reported that the building was haunted by many spirits, including two that he and his wife witnessed at close range. Whilst sitting in their parlour, they heard noises in the hall, and they had made their way out to the stairs, only to be confronted with the apparitions of an Edwardian couple, to whom they got within touching distance before they disappeared from sight. A strange addition to their experience was that the vicar described them both as having skin the colour and texture of elephant hide! Could this Edwardian man have been responsible for David's frightening moment? Another tale that is particularly interesting when compared to David's story, is that of another vicar living in the rectory, who once fled from the building after hearing a voice saying to him 'Why don't you turn around and look at me?' – not the very same words as those spoken to David, but very nearly, and the gist is definitely the same.

The Gower Heritage Centre, Parkmill

The peninsula of Gower is fifteen miles long and only about six miles wide, although in the past the area of Gower also included a lot of land to the north-east. While many people have heard of the 'Little England beyond England' in South Pembrokeshire, Gower remains a mystery. Up until the outbreak of the Second World War, it remained largely a region of small farming communities with its own dialect and traditions. Its unique character was forged from its mix of Welsh, Somerset/North Devon and Norman ancestry, and the dialect was similar to that of people from the West Country.

Gower was divided into the area of the Welsh (Welsherie) in the north, which was where Welsh was spoken (for example, the areas of Penclawdd and Llanrhidian), and the English (Gower)-speaking districts, which were located from the south of Gower to Llangennith in the north-west.

It was during the twelfth century that the Le Breos family, who were granted sovereignty by King John in 1203, established Parc Le Breos, a deer park of about 500 acres on land to the west of Parkmill, used for both deer hunting and military training. It was here that they built a corn mill.

The Gower Heritage Centre.

Our story begins on a normal Saturday in March 2004, and it had been cold and miserable with constant rain. Grant had a fairly quiet morning, not getting up until 10 a.m. and then busying himself getting ready to join a friend's paranormal group at the Gower Heritage Centre for an overnight event. Grant was not really all that interested in the subject and was only going to keep his friend company and provide moral support. He made sure that he had the basics: a torch, good shoes and waterproof clothing due to much of the site being outdoors. His friend had stated that no alcohol was allowed to be consumed prior to the event, so Grant had not gone out drinking the night before to ensure that there was nothing in his system and that if anything occurred he would know it was real.

The evening was very quiet with nothing really happening. Dowsing had only produced the stream nearby, and EVP had recorded some very active ducks. The ouija board had produced a few interesting results but nothing which could be confirmed at the time. Grant was in a group with two other people who he did not know, and although introductions had been made, he was never very good with names and could not remember who they were.

As this was his first voyage into the world of the paranormal, he was quite nervous when attempting such tasks as calling out or using the ouija board; in fact he was very nervous for the early part of the night, until he became used to the way things worked and the technical language that everyone else seemed to be using.

After an hour's break for food at midnight, they went back to various pieces of scientific equipment that had been brought and tried to use those. For example, Grant had an Electro-Magnetic Field Detector (EMF) which, after walking around the entire centre and mill, had produced no results. The teams then split up again to continue with their small group work, and Grant and the two ladies with him went to investigate the stream and the mill.

The lane leading to what was once 'Devil's Row'.

After conducting another EVP session in the mill and spending the best part of an hour attempting to contact the old miller, they decided to give up. As they were making their way to the stream using the outside route, they suddenly stopped open-mouthed, as the figure of a woman could clearly be seen running into the trees near the stream.

The figure of the lady in a long dress was being followed very quickly by that of a shadowy black silhouette with no real form, and both figures disappeared into the trees as quickly as they had appeared. Grant and his fellow team mates decided that they had seen and experienced enough for the night after this, and all left immediately without even telling the other group they were going. Grant has and never will set foot in the Gower Heritage Centre again or will he ever join his friend to investigate the paranormal.

This experience is a particularly interesting one, because it does actually tie in very nicely with a piece of known history of the area, something paranormal investigators are always looking for. Unfortunately, we are unable to tell you this history because of its use on Gower Heritage Centre events, but maybe if you ever attend one of their ghostly events, you will find the connection yourselves.

Our next experience with the Gower Heritage Centre was in the spring of 2008. Steve and Clare had been contacted by Chance Encounters Heritage Interpretation Theatre Co. at very short notice to provide a short paranormal investigation-based murder mystery at the centre due to a change of booking. When they arrived, they discussed the evening with the manager and decided that the visiting guests would be split into three groups and then spend a section of the evening with each of them. The manager would first explain about the murder they were investigating (based on a true story connected with the site). Then they would spend a session with Steve doing EVP in the air-raid shelter by the mill, a session with Clare learning the art of dowsing down by the stream, and a session with the manager learning more of the history of the site.

When the guests arrived, including a number of children of all ages, they split into groups and started the evening's events. The following tale comes from the first group to do EVP with Steve. After explaining what EVP was all about and how to do it, they passed the tape around introducing themselves, leaving a gap for any possible spirits to leave a reply. The group seemed fascinated by the experiment, and all took it very seriously, including the children who were as quiet as mice throughout. On listening back to the tape, after one member of the group, Michelle, introduced herself, they all heard a very clear voice whispering 'Devil's Row' – clear enough that they all agreed on the words, but none of them knew what it meant if anything! Steve has been doing EVP experiments for a long time now, and knows to make a verbal note on the tape if anyone speaks when they are not meant to, or if a sound is heard that they know has a natural explanation, and he knows for sure that on this occasion this voice did not come from one of the group. He was also quite amazed at the clarity of the voice because, as Steve will readily admit, listening back to EVP tapes is not a skill he has managed to develop, and always leaves it to others to take on this role.

At the end of the night, when the whole group were feeding back their experiences, very few of which were worthy of note, this group told the manager of their EVP experience. They were quite shocked, to say the least, when he clearly knew of a connection. He went on to explain that there was a row of old cottages up on the hill above the mill, once known on the old Tithe map as 'Devil's Row'!

The Mumbles Pier, Mumbles

Mumbles Pier was originally built and opened on 10 May 1898, designed by W. Sutcliffe Marsh. It was commissioned as the terminus for the Swansea to Mumbles railway. Frequented by the many steelworkers and miners living in the area, the pier was popular for its regular steamer excursions to other resorts on the Welsh coast, along with the resorts of North Devon and Somerset. It has a simple pitch-pine deck upon lattice steelwork. Piers became popular during the Victorian era, and although Mumbles Pier was not as ornate and did not have as many of the usual attractions of other piers of its day, it was still a popular tourist attraction.

In 1916, a slipway was added for the RNLI lifeboat and in 1922 a lifeboat house was added and is still used today. The pier is very much still a popular tourist attraction. There are many amusement arcades, a skating rink and excellent fishing facilities from the pier itself. For a building with such happy connotations and history, it is not well renowned for its spooky goings on. However, there has been one incident that certainly can't easily be explained.

Mr David Morgan of Gendros recalls a strange incident one evening, long after the pier was shut to the public:

> I had arrived at the pier area at about 1 a.m. As a father to a teenage daughter, I often found myself waiting in strange places at ungodly hours to pick her up, and this particular day was no different. My daughter was attending a party at the local pier nightclub and I had gone, as usual, to act as her free taxi service. It was a cold and crisp evening in November, and I

Clock at the entrance of the Mumbles Pier.

View looking down the Mumbles Pier.

A postcard showing the Mumbles Pier as it once was.

remember it was a surprisingly clear evening. I remember looking up at the stars and full moon and seeing them with such clarity.

After enjoying the solitude for a while, I glanced across the pier and saw what appeared to be a lady. She was wearing a long dress and what looked like a shawl or scarf covering her head, and she was walking away from me towards the end of the pier. I thought this strange because I knew that the pier was closed for the evening and being so late and cold the last thing I expected was to find other people wandering around, although, I guess, to have found other parents acting as taxi service to the local teenagers would have been quite likely. Slightly perplexed as to why such a primly dressed woman would be there, I continued to watch as she walked to the end of the pier. As she reached the end, she started to walk from left to right, and then very suddenly she turned around and started walking back towards the entrance. This is when things took a turn for the unusual.

I continued watching her as I thought that she might be in trouble and may have needed help of some sort. Suddenly, in front of my eyes, she just sort of faded away. I walked nearer to the entrance to the pier to see if I could catch a glimpse of her again but she had vanished. She did not walk past me and when I got to the gates of the pier they were firmly shut.

I don't know what I saw that night but I still remember it vividly to this day.

Who or why was the lady visiting the pier at such an ungodly hour? This we may never know, but it certainly gave David something to think about that night.

Newton House, Dinefwr Park, Llandeilo.

Newton House, Llandeilo

Val Williams, SWPR patron and proprietor of Chance Encounters Heritage Interpretation Theatre Co., visits her fair share of locations throughout South Wales. One of the locations she frequents is Newton House in Dinefwr Park, Llandeilo.

Newton House, built in 1660 but now with a Victorian façade and a fountain garden, is at the heart of Dinefwr Park. There had been a manor house on the ancestral estate since the fifteenth century but it was in 1775, at the time of the creation of the 1st Baron, that the grounds were remodelled by Capability Brown in the fashion of the time – a carefully controlled 'wilderness' of sweeping parkland punctuated by groups of towering trees. The grounds are famous for their medieval deer park, and home to more than 100 fallow deer. Stroll back through the deer park and you soon arrive at Newton House (or Plas Dinefwr), the 'new' castle. Although the present Newton House dates back to 1660 and Sir Edward Rice – fifth generation grandfather of the present Lord Dynevor – the house has substantial eighteenth-century and Victorian Gothic additions.

Newton House has had something of an unhappy recent history. It was sold by the present Lord Dynevor in 1974 and suffered badly, falling into near ruinous disrepair. It was occupied by squatters for many years and was stripped of many of its original features. Mercifully, both the medieval castle and Newton House have recently been restored by Cadw and the National Trust respectively.

Dinefwr Castle, overlooking Newton House.

This is Val's story:

Although I work in haunted sites on a regular basis, there is only one where I believe that I have felt something genuinely unpleasant. Much as I love this property, there is one area of it where I would not be prepared to spend the night alone under virtually any circumstances [and this from someone who is regularly locked up in Llancaiach Fawr Manor House on her own].

We had been doing a Victorian weekend there for the National Trust. It had been a really pleasant weekend and when we were offered the chance to see the parts of the house not normally open to the public, we leapt at the chance.

At this stage, I knew the house was reputedly haunted but the only tales I had heard related to Lord Walter. When we reached the uppermost floor, there was a certain atmosphere but nothing oppressive. I still can't explain my reaction when we reached a certain point. One of the regular staff who witnessed it still says it was as though I had walked into a brick wall. He also says that I lost my colour and looked physically sick. The only way I can describe it was that I was knocked off balance by a feeling of actual evil (however melodramatic that may sound). Not only did I refuse to go any further, I refused point blank to let any of my co-workers go there either. Later I found out that two other women in the group also felt something at the same point and that a previous worker there had had similar experiences.

I now do ghost tours on the site and it still takes all my courage to turn my back to the same doorway.

While researching for the tours I was pointed in the direction of an old story relating to the house. It seems that in the eighteenth century, Lady Elinor Cavendish – a relative of the mistress of the house – sought sanctuary there, seeking to hide from an unwanted suitor. Her presence was discovered by her would-be lover who found her and killed her. Apparently, a maidservant who witnessed the crime hanged herself in one of the rooms in the upper part of the house (or perhaps she was a second victim?). I don't know if this crime was related to the over-powering emotions that I experienced but I am certain that something happened that has left behind a very unpleasant residue.

Swansea Museum, Swansea Town Centre

This is not so much a ghost story, but it is rather odd. Swansea Museum is the oldest museum in Wales. It was opened in 1841 by a group of local people who were known as The Royal Institution of South Wales, which gave the museum building its original name. In 1991, Swansea City Council took over the running of the museum, and began renovation of the building.

Val Williams, who has just recounted her rather uncomfortable experience in Newton House, tells us a tale of miraculous coincidences:

> One of the many places that I work is Swansea Museum. Years ago, it was decided to base some school sessions around paintings in the collection that are, quite unusually, of ordinary people. In two of them there is a female figure that could easily be the same person. Although nothing was known about her identity, it was decided to make her someone from the 1851 census. Since one of the paintings was of Morris Lane, we looked at the census

Swansea Museum.

The artistic fountain in the centre of Swansea.

returns for that street. Alice Francis was chosen only because, at the time, she was the closest to me in age.

Since all we knew about Alice came from that one census, we had to make up a biography for her to fill in the gaps. We began doing the sessions and as a result I was asked to do an adult version for the Royal Institution. When it was advertised, I was actually contacted by the direct descendant of one of Alice's sisters. From her family, I discovered more about her past and this is where it began to get a bit strange. There was not one detail in her fictional biography that did not fit. Some things were not known one way or the other, but from the place of her birth to the number of her sisters and from her earlier occupation to a late romance, everything was right.

This could just be down to her being created to be 'typical' of the time but it became even more coincidental. It turned out that one of her sisters actually worked for the patron of the artist William Butler and was working in Burrows Lodge at the time the artist was staying there.

To add to the coincidences, I was ill on one occasion and my colleague, Tony, had to stand in as a friend of Alice's. He made up a character who was a former mariner who was now a copper-worker. When the census was checked, a man of the same name lived in the street Tony had chosen and was a copper-worker!

Three

HAUNTINGS IN THE WORKPLACE

For most of us, the building we work in is one that we spend far more time in than we would often like, so it would make sense that many people's brush with the paranormal is whilst they are at work. For those working in pubs or hotels, for example, we may well be spending the larger part of our week in a building that is hundreds of years old and steeped in history. If we take the theory that states that much paranormal activity is a historical recording, stored in the fabric of a building, we must assume that many of these sites have many a tale to tell.

In this chapter we tell you of a number of unfortunate employees who have received more than they bargained for when they accepted their job offer, and we begin with a story set in the Welsh mines, and therefore a very important part of Welsh industrial heritage.

Afan Mines, Afan Valley

Miners are generally a superstitious lot and are often reluctant to talk about any unusual occurrences either underground or above it. Many miners were born and brought up in the Afan Valley; fathers, sons and brothers all worked at sometime underground, and it was mainly these former miners who recounted the stories. For those unfamiliar with this part of South Wales, this valley reaches like a crooked finger from Port Talbot into the uplands that serve as a backdrop to the flat coastal area of Swansea Bay. It is hard to believe that in living history this was a valley full of factories working metal, and of course a myriad of collieries both large and small. This is one of many areas of Glamorgan that suffered the ravages of the Industrial Revolution, and is only now returning to something like the unspoilt countryside that it once must have been. However, coal has been mined hereabouts since at least the Middle Ages, and underneath its green exterior the land is riddled with pits and levels. Like any folklore, the

A view looking down the Afan Valley.

stories regarding supernatural phenomena are difficult to date, but it can be assumed that most occurred between the mid-nineteenth and twentieth centuries when the coal industry was at its peak in the Afan Valley. Injury and death were commonplace in the early days. However, the risk increased again in the Depression as out-of-work miners ventured into old workings without adequate protection and using methods they knew were unsafe. When one has a choice between feeding the family and taking risks, there was often no option. However, there were many instances where a strange incident or spectral beings warned the miners of impending dangers and often saved their lives. Of course, from this point in time it is often possible to come up with plausible explanations for some mysterious phenomena, but others are still in the realm of the unexplained. So let us go into the underworld that is probably one of the most dangerous workplaces in the principality.

On the opposite side of the river just above Pontryhdyfen, on the edge of what is now Afan Argoed Country Park, were a series of levels stretching deep into the hillside. By the 1920s most of these workings had been abandoned in favour of the larger deep mines, but with the onset of the Depression, unemployed miners often unofficially worked these levels by hand. This was usually a covert operation involving a miner working alone, or in pairs, hauling out their coal by hand in a simple wooden dram. This incident concerned a father and son, and occurred when the latter was busy hauling out a full dram. The father returned to the coalface and turned to see a figure beckoning him in the gloom. At first he thought it was his son returning to tell him of some problem, but as he approached the figure he began to notice that it had its

A view looking up the Afan Valley.

own eerie glow and then it suddenly disappeared. Almost immediately there was a roar behind him and the roof of the seam where he was just working caved in. This is just one of many tales from the area where an unexplained spectre or incident has warned of impending disasters. Some miners took heed of the warnings whilst others did not and suffered the consequences.

Further down the valley on the same side was another drift mine, where much more sinister happenings eventually forced it to be abandoned. Phantom dogs are supernatural phenomena found all over the country, but this is the only one where it is said they appear underground. Again, most sightings of these spectral beasts describe them as being black in colour, although eyewitness reports claim that this one was a reddish brown. Some miners reported seeing this snarling spectre with fiery red eyes bounding towards them through the entrance tunnel and many refused to work there again. One worker even claimed that this spectre resembled a fire-breathing dragon, but there is no record of how much he had to drink before entering the mine!

There were also numerous reports of whisperings and eerie lights floating through many of these levels and were usually a precursor to a roof fall, collapse or gas explosion. Whether or not there is a guardian spirit of coalminers is open to debate, but at least these phenomena were effective at warning miners of impending danger. Recent research has come up with a scientific reason for such activity. Geopathic stress in rock formations is now known to generate energy that can manifest itself as lights; could movement of the seams prior to a collapse be generating such spectres? Trapped gas also makes a noise very much like a low whistling sound as it escapes into the workings and this may be the source of the alleged whisperings. Whatever the answer is, this advanced warning, when heeded, has saved many a life.

The last story from the Afan Valley is not about the mines, but it is about the mysterious disappearance of a miner. Like many unsolved mysteries, the incident evoked ancient folklore of the area. An elderly inhabitant of Cwmavon told this tale that in turn was passed down to him by his grandmother. As children, he and his siblings had been warned to stay away from the River Afan, lest the White Lady lure them into her drowning pool. Like the sirens of Greek mythology and the maiden of the Lorelei on the Rhine, this spectre was said to entice the unwary into a particularly dangerous part of this South Wales river. Some said that your fate depended on this apparition's mood, as sometimes she would guide travellers unfamiliar with the area to a safe crossing place or on other occasions to probable death. You will not find it named on any modern maps; however, Pwll Gwen Marw or the White Pool of Death was believed to be on the River Afon by the village of Cwmavon. The pool was probably a cavity caused by a restriction of the river at this point and soft rock easily eroded. It is said that the river was unusually deep at this location, and both current and depth increased the dangers. The way the river undercut the rocks also meant that it was easy for the unwary to get trapped. Despite all the warnings, it was common in the summer for miners, after their hot and dirty work, to bathe in these cool and refreshing waters. A pile of work clothes on the bank was the only evidence that this unknown miner had entered the pool of death. His body was never found and thus he entered the local folklore as yet another victim of the White Lady of the Afon.

Gorseinon Hospital, Gorseinon

Gorseinon is situated in a lovely area of the Swansea valleys between Swansea and Llanelli. Hidden away in its heart, Gorseinon Hospital was opened in 1930 as a gift to the people of Gorseinon from William Rufus Lewis JP. Once its doors opened, it welcomed its first matron to take charge of the hospital, Jane Thomas, and it started life as a small community hospital, with a children's ward, maternity ward, a minor operating theatre and a casualty department.

During the period from 1930 to 1948, the Gorseinon Hospital Entertainments Committee was formed, and people were appointed to this committee from all different walks of life, the sole purpose being to provide for the patients and staff of the hospital. Ladies formed a linen guild, and provided linen for the wards. Local people donated beds, armchairs, curtains and toys for the children's ward. It was a fantastic example of true Welsh community spirit. This local support enabled the hospital to continue providing its valuable service to the people.

In 1948, the Health Service was nationalised and all hospitals became part of the state. The old entertainments committee now came to an end, as their constitution only covered a 'private'-type hospital, which Gorseinon used to be, having been donated by Rufus Lewis and being maintained by private patronage. Therefore, Gorseinon Hospital is no longer in private ownership and is now part of the Division of Medicine and Elderly Care. It has a total of sixty-six beds, forty-four of which provide assessment and rehabilitation of the elderly. The remaining twenty-two beds provide intermediate care, including six designated for arthroplasty patients, and the unit is well supported by a multidisciplinary team.

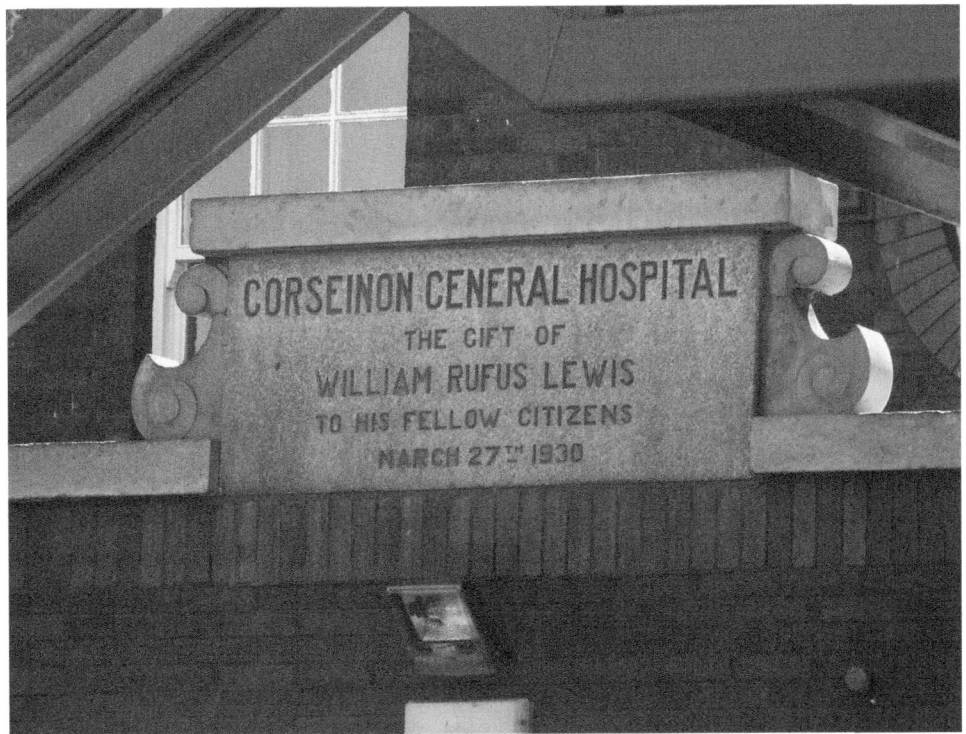

The stone plaque above the entrance of Gorseinon Hospital.

The hospital has a small outpatients department, which hosts a variety of clinics including ENT, orthopaedic, diabetic, elderly care and gynaecology. There are also nurse-led urology and obstetrics clinics. Local general practitioners have direct access to x-ray, phlebotomy and physiotherapy outpatient services. The unit hosts the Community Rehabilitation Enablement Team (CREST) and the Sure Start team which are part of the Divisions of Diagnostics, Therapeutics and Community Services. As you can see, Gorseinon Hospital still works extremely hard as it continues to provide the high levels of care it has striven to achieve.

With its rich heritage spanning such a long period of time, it is no wonder that its walls have been known to witness a number of strange occurrences. If you subscribe to the popular theory that much paranormal activity is directly linked to high levels of emotion and activity over a period of time, becoming ingrained in the fabric of a building, what better place than a busy community hospital?

In 2003 at 4.30 a.m., Daniel recalls a very unnerving experience that has stayed very much in his thoughts, and he told us of the following incident:

I had just finished attending to a patient, and I stood by the sink in the ward. I proceeded to wash my hands, something that I am obviously doing on a very regular basis. As I glanced up and towards the office door, I saw a strange figure that gave me reason to pause. It looked like a woman, and the figure was not quite solid, but neither was it transparent. I picked up some towels and started walking towards the office whilst drying my hands, my rational side having kicked in

Gorseinon Hospital.

and now assuming that she was just a patient wandering around and maybe a little confused. As I got closer to the office, the figure moved towards the kitchen and then moved towards a cubicle and disappeared. Being by this time a little nervous, I made a full check of the area, only to find that all staff and patients were fully accounted for at that time. To this very day I still have no explanation for the mysterious woman I witnessed, but I am sure I will never forget her.

In the following June of 2004, Lisa remembers a very strange experience of her own, and tells us this story:

I was seeing to a patient in cubicle 2 with a staff nurse, and we sat the patient up for her to drink her tea in comfort. The cot sides were attached firmly to the bed and were in the up position, and the patient was watching and enjoying some of the Wimbledon Tennis Championships on the television which was situated near the door. The other member of staff and I walked away from the bed and towards the television, and both of us were sneakily watching little bits of the tennis. Suddenly, back in cubicle 2, the right-hand cot side started to shake violently back and forth, and we stopped and stared at it as it continued to shake for about fifteen seconds before suddenly coming to a stop. Needless to say we did not stick around to watch the rest of the match, but we never did manage to explain the events of that afternoon.

Lisa also recalled another brief experience:

> I was on night duty and I had collected the patients' menus together and put them behind the desk in the corridor. I walked away checking that all the doors were securely locked and that there were no windows open, which proved to be fine. However, about an hour later I walked down the corridor to answer a buzzer only to find all the menus had been scattered all over the corridor.

Was there a spirit making a statement about the hospital food perhaps?

Another ex-staff member was on night duty and had a rather memorable moment. He clearly remembers shutting down the ward for the night and unplugging the radio in the kitchen from the mains socket before going about his usual business. Things took a change for the bizarre when a few hours later he could hear music playing. Thinking that a patient had put on a radio by their bed perhaps he went to investigate only to find that the radio in the kitchen had been plugged back in and was switched on, and no patients had left their beds or staff entered the area.

These accounts are the ones that have been reported to us, but this does not mean, of course, that is the extent of the activity. Many people experiencing phenomena of this kind may well not tell anyone for fear of ridicule, or as a way to try and convince themselves that it did not really happen. For all we know these events could be occurring on a regular basis! What we do know so far is that most of the reported activity in Gorseinon Hospital seems to occur in cubicle 2 or its vicinity. Very strange indeed.

Tesco Supermarket, Bridgend Town Centre

Castles, old buildings, crash sites, houses, all locations you may be unsurprised to hear stories of alleged hauntings and ghostly encounters. But how many of us have ever heard of a haunted supermarket?

Richard had heard many stories, from various members of staff, that the supermarket in which he worked was haunted. Richard, who at that point had been with the supermarket for two and a half years, had heard that some staff had experienced strange goings on within the building, which lays the foundation for this story.

It was 30 October 2005, and the supermarket was holding a charity spooky sleepover in the store for staff members. The evening started off in the supermarket's warehouse, with everyone together talking about the variety of unexplained experiences different people had had. A local medium was invited to the evening and was with the group in the warehouse at this time. It had been arranged so that everyone who was on site would be gathered together in this part of the building, ensuring that the rest of the store was empty.

Suddenly, whilst everyone stood around in the warehouse, the public address system, which is used to make announcements in the store, turned on for around ten seconds and then turned off! The system has a push button microphone which is located on the customer service desk on the other side of the supermarket. Who pressed the button? Everyone was together in the warehouse, and as there was not a single person anywhere near the customer service desk, this was just a little weird!

The mysterious picture taken inside Tesco supermarket – what do you see?

The discussion continued for a short while longer, until the group decided to start a walk around the store. The medium joined them, ready to tell the intrepid investigators about anything he might pick up as they were on their travels. The first location was the bakery. Upon entering the area, the medium started to pick up some information. He said that before the supermarket had been built twenty-five years earlier, there had been a bakery exactly on the site of the supermarket's bakery now! Rather disturbingly he went on to explain that he felt that someone had once hung themselves in the bakery. Was it the old bakery or the new bakery? This we are unsure of as the medium was unable to distinguish at the time.

The next part of the building the group travelled to was the main shop floor. Before the store had been built, this specific area of land had been the site of a cattle market. The medium stated that he could see a woman, who wore period dress, walking around the area. Upon further questioning he explained that she seemed to be from the time of the cattle market. This woman, according to the medium, was named Mary, but no further information was obtained.

On another part of the shop floor, the medium once again picked up on a 'spirit'. He said that this 'spirit' was a customer from the supermarket. He said that this woman had enjoyed her times shopping, so that is why she came back to the place. Funnily enough, the location in which the medium indicated that this spiritual customer frequented has had a fair share of strange things reported – mainly packets being rustled on the shelves and glass jars being knocked together.

The next location was the store's training room, which was on the first floor. The medium sensed that there was a gentleman in the room. Other than that there was very little information that he could obtain at this point. Interestingly, when the store has been shut and locked up for the night, a gentleman has been seen looking out of the window by various members of staff.

When venturing back inside, the staff never managed to find this mysterious apparition.

After the intriguing walk about, people were split into three groups, which were then sent to three locations throughout the store. The locations were the back staircase, the bakery and the shop floor.

Richard and his group were first sent to the back staircase. The stairs are made of marble, with the walls of the staircase being solid concrete. Nothing specific was experienced by his group in the back stairs. However, some people in the past have reported having strange but powerful sensations in that area. As true investigators, the group deduced that this could probably be explained because the staircase is steep, it is very cold in the area and there is not much lighting. Combined, these could create a form of sense deprivation, producing a natural feeling of uneasiness.

The next location for Richard and his team was the bakery. From a paranormal point of view, this location started off very well. Very soon taps and raps were being heard in all the corners of the bakery. Upon investigation the group discovered that there was no machinery turned on, so as far as they were concerned, the noises could not be fully explained.

The final location was the shop floor, but unfortunately nothing happened during this time. By the time the groups had visited all three locations, it was 1.30 a.m. After a fifteen-minute break, there were only a few brave investigators left, as many people had become tired and decided to go home.

With the fearless few left, it was decided to spend the remaining time on the shop floor. After exploring and investigating the different parts of the area, the group finally arrived at the pet food aisle at around 2.45 a.m. Fifteen minutes later, while the group talked quietly amongst themselves, they all started to hear what can only be described as rustling. The noise started on the crisp aisle with crisp packets, then moved onto the tea and coffee aisle, where jars of coffee could be heard banging against each other, with glass clinking against glass. Soon after one of the members of the group, Janet, suddenly became very ill and without any warning ran to the checkouts to the nearest bin to be sick. It was at this point that it was decided to call it a night!

During the evening, Richard had been taking many photographs with his digital camera, and he had continued during his time in the bakery. One particular photograph was of the doors that led into the bakery. After reviewing the photos of the night, this photo stood out.

When looking carefully at the picture, Richard noticed that there appeared to be something unusual in the window. During the whole night, the lights inside this particular set of doors were turned on for safety and they could be seen in all of the other photographs. But not in this one: what can you see?

Pontardawe Inn, Pontardawe

Deep in the Swansea valley, nestled amongst the hills, you will find the little village of Pontardawe, which when translated into English means 'Bridge over the River Tawe'. Pontardawe first came into existence as a settlement between two drovers' tracks; one from Swansea to Brecon, and the second from Neath to Llandeilo. Pontardawe, during the latter part of the eighteenth century, and up to the middle part of the nineteenth century, was mainly an industrial area with the majority of its inhabitants working in either the steel or tinplate works which transported goods all over the world. Pontardawe is no longer a busy

The sign at the Pontadawe Inn.

industrial area but is now a tranquil and beautiful mountainous locality. Pontardawe's best-known landmark is the spire of St Peter's Church, which sits on a high point close to the centre of the village and overlooks the Swansea Canal.

Music now holds a very important part in the life of all the people who live there, and Pontardawe holds an annual music festival, where musicians come from across the globe to share their talents. Pontardawe's festival organisation kindly renovated the dilapidated Pontardawe Inn (Y Gwachel to locals) in 1995, and it is in this very quaint and lonely old alehouse that our story takes place.

Y Gwachel occupies the site of what once was a much older alehouse that was situated on the old Drovers' road, which leads onto a small stone bridge – the very bridge from which Pontardawe derives its name. The bridge was completed in the 1760s and originally had steps which were only accessible to humans and animals, and it was then smoothed over and doubled in width to allow access for carts. Under the bridge sits a strange engraving on one of the

The Pontadawe Inn, as seen from the road above.

stones, the engraving of a witch on a broomstick, which in some circles in Welsh explains the name Y Gwachel, or 'witches coven'.

With the inn being over 250 years old, and a mixture of both public dwelling during the Second World War and public house, it has a lot of history. It contains some of the original bread ovens in the cellar, and has a wonderful flight of semi-circular stone steps, which undoubtedly has seen some form of paranormal activity.

There have been many strange happenings and the following are just a few which have been reported to us by the current owners, Hywel and Beth.

Hywel was sitting in his office in the cellar, after the inn had closed, counting up the day's takings. Not really paying attention to his surroundings, and deeply concentrating on the job at hand, he was suddenly aware of being watched. Upon looking up he was disturbed to see the sight of a white figure, approximately the height of a small child. The entity walked straight through the table at which he was sitting and through the opposite wall. Hywel quickly jumped up to check the room adjoining the one in which he was working, but no one could be seen.

This next incident was reported in the main bar, has happened on many different occasions throughout the years since Hywel and Beth became owners, and has been experienced by both staff and customers. This particular occurrence was witnessed by a member of staff who we shall call Julie. As far as she was concerned, it was a usual working day, attending to the needs of any customers who entered the inn. She was standing behind the bar when suddenly, without warning, a glass flew off the top shelf and started to spin wildly on the floor! Stunned and perturbed by the flying glass, she reported it to her colleagues. She then discovered that this had happened many times, at all times of day or night but with variations; glasses from the second or third row have been seen to do the same thing. The most unusual thing is that the floor behind the bar is solid stone, so any glasses that are dropped from the top shelf should, and in normal circumstances would, have smashed on contact.

The next story involves a mysterious visitor to the inn. It had again been a normal day for Hywel and Beth, until in walked someone they did not recognise. She certainly wasn't one of their regulars. The lady approached them and told them that she used to live there during the Second World War as an evacuee, and asked if they minded if she looked around for old time's sake. Of course they agreed, but after a while she asked whether they minded if she had a look downstairs. She went on to explain that this was once the area where the main house used to be, and it was her job every morning to clean and light the fire. The unknown lady went on to tell Hywel that almost every morning when carrying out this task, she would clean the grate and lay the sticks ready. She would then walk outside to get the coal, but each time on her return the sticks had been removed from the fire and thrown across the floor.

The last story takes place on a rather quiet day in February 2008. It had been a normal day for Hywel, Beth and their staff. They had set up the bar ready for the busy evening ahead, and had seen a few customers who had already been served their lunchtime meals and drinks. When Hywel was standing in the bar attending to customers he suddenly heard barrels being moved around in the cellar. Knowing that all staff were accounted for and that he, personally, had closed and double-bolted the door after last going down there, he was just a little curious as to how on earth someone had managed to get in. Walking down the stairs into the room leading onto the cellar, he noticed that all the bolts were still locked. Unlocking them all, he entered the cellar. To his complete surprise, there was no one there and all the barrels of ale remained stacked in their original place, begging the question what was creating the sounds Hywel had heard so clearly? There are variations of this occurrence which have been reported by other members of staff. All staff, as a rule of the inn, ensure that both bolts are in place before leaving the cellar. On numerous occasions they have returned only to find that one of the bolts have been opened. Who is this mystery visitor to the Pontardawe Inn's cellars? We would love to hear from any person who has a theory that may be linked to the inn's past.

A Mumbles B&B, Mumbles

A mere five miles outside Swansea city centre lies the busy coastal town of Mumbles. This town of restaurants, small art galleries and craft shops, the beautiful beaches which include

A view of Mumbles Bay.

Bracelet and Limeslade, and the unmissible Mumbles Pier, is commonly known as the gateway to the Gower. Mumbles has Oystermouth Castle standing proudly on its banks, so steeped in history with many tragedies and natural disasters, it is no wonder that paranormal activity is rife in the area.

On 30 January 1607, Mumbles was the scene of death and destruction, when around 9 a.m. a tsunami hit the coastline and killed hundreds of people. It is in this location 400 years later that an unnamed Mumbles B&B is experiencing some quite exceptional paranormal activity. The B&B is situated on one of the quiet side streets, and from the exterior looks just like every other house on the block, but inside a very different story plays out.

There are many stories linked to this building and the following are just a few things that the owner Heather Davies described to us. She and her son Gary moved into the house in 2002, and prior to them converting it into a B&B it was used as flats. The first strange occurrence was on a very normal day when Heather and four other people were in her kitchen, situated at the back of the building. As they stood around chatting away, they were all amazed when all five of them witnessed Gary's sock being thrown by some invisible force from the kitchen table and across the room. Strange, but true.

On a separate occasion, Heather placed a pair of knitting needles on the coffee table. Soon after, when she went to walk out from the room to head for the kitchen, she heard a ping. On turning back and investigating this sudden sound, she found the plastic top of one of the knitting needles had managed to unglue itself from the main needle and had hit the radiator, landing at her feet. At first thought you may be thinking that there is nothing exceptionally unusual about this event, but the strange fact is that the knitting needles were angled with the point of the needle facing the radiator, so somehow the plastic tip must have turned in mid-air and doubled backed on itself to hit the radiator.

Another experience very similar to the one described above occurred in Gary's bedroom on the middle floor of the house. Gary is a very normal twenty-year-old young man, and on speaking to him about his strange and frightening story, he seemed very sensible and not at all the type to lie or make things up. Whilst practicing with his darts in his room one evening after a long day, he threw a dart only to see the dart stop in mid-air, turn around and head back towards him. Gary threw himself on the bed very quickly with the dart narrowly missing his head.

In addition to the above events, on regular intervals a ghostly presence can be sensed and heard roaming around the B&B, walking up and down the staircase. Could this unknown presence also be affecting the electricity we wonder, because on numerous occasions the fire alarms (which are tested regularly) suddenly start to go off by themselves, and this always seems to happen when Heather and Gary are not in the house and they arrive home to find the alarms ringing. Lights have also been known to turn on and off when there is no one near a light switch. To add to the mystery, the electric wiring has been fully checked by professional electricians who can find no fault in any part of the building.

Our last tale from this spooky B&B concerns a mysterious little girl, who has been seen many times on the ground floor of the building. She seems to enjoy appearing mainly to male visitors. Two of the people that have seen her have independently described her as 'a very pale-faced little girl of about eleven, with long dark hair', and the final eerie detail, 'with an evil or mischievous-looking face'.

Whatever the explanation for this host of strange happenings, one would imagine that this particular B&B would lead to a memorable and eventful stay!

Four

PERSONAL AND PRIVATE PHENOMENA

Although many of the long-known ghost stories are connected with huge buildings and historic locations, many of us have encountered strange and frightening moments in the warmth and comfort of our own home, the one place we hope to feel most safe.

Most of us would admit to having experienced some of the more basic forms of paranormal phenomena at home, things such as knowing who is on the telephone before we pick it up, but some people have been subjected to far more direct and unsettling memories. In this chapter we recount the experiences of a number of witnesses from their family home, beginning with a very eerie tale that spans a considerable period of time in the life of one young man.

Strange Events at Alma Terrace, Ogmore Vale

'Sinister' is the word applied to the atmosphere generated by the house our next witness, Krys, lived in during the late 1940s to early 1960s. It was a typical terraced two-bedroom property, which his father bought from the Coal Board, and his parents went to live there in Ogmore Vale just after the Second World War. The house, one of five in the terrace, at that time cost the princely sum of £250, bought on his coalminer's wage of £4 a week.

Although Krys's father pioneered many improvements to the property, such as adding a bathroom, and an early version of a 'conservatory', the sense of oppression felt in the house was so strong, it has been with him all these years.

The house had been lived in before they took possession, but it was very run-down and needed work to restore it. Years later, they learned that a man had taken his own life, either in the house or in the one next door, by gas poisoning.

Alma Terrace, Ogmore Vale.

Krys's brother, Mike, who is five years older, also judged the house sinister and dark. They came to independent judgements on this and had never actually shared their feelings about the house until much later, in the late 1980s. The startling thing was that their strange experiences turned out to be very similar.

Looking back at their memories, they are one of fear – Krys would try to be the one who washed up after dinner, rather than the one drying the dishes, because that meant being left alone in the kitchen when everyone else was in the lounge, including the budgerigar, Jimmy. There was something very sinister about the kitchen and 'conservatory' area, as there was about the top left-hand bedroom in the terraced house.

However, three specific incidents in the house stand out in Krys's memory.

The room he had as his own was the smaller of two on the first floor. He must have been aged about eight (in 1956) when he suddenly woke early one morning, and sat bolt upright. He turned his head to the right and saw a tall, white shape at the end of the room. It did not move but just stood there. This shape must have been about 6ft in height. Krys was terrified and just froze, then he hid under the bedclothes.

Over the years, until they left Ogmore Vale for Sydney, Australia, in 1964, he was to experience some further types of sensation in that room – of someone stroking his hair, of the bed shaking, of an oppression in the room, and nightmares. In one instance, a voice said, 'There's a ghost in this house.' There was not one night that he slept easily, and spent most of the time under the blankets. Krys absolutely hated the dark of the room and would never venture downstairs at night.

His brother had had that room as a bedroom before Krys was born. It was only in the late 1980s that they shared views of what they each had experienced at that house. Krys asked him of his experiences in that particular room, and the reply was, 'Oh, it was sinister. Things like the bed shaking.'

It was in about 1962 that an eerie incident at their house in Alma Terrace involved his parents. He was asleep and was not to know of their experience that night until years later. By then his brother had joined the RAF and was living in England.

Mary and Howard were friends of Krys's parents and lived opposite. They emigrated to Australia in about 1959. Friends they then made in Sydney visited Britain in 1962 and came down to Wales for a week, where they stayed with Krys's family.

There were five in their party altogether – the Johnstons, daughters Cheryl and Bindi (a part-Aboriginal adopted daughter), and Cheryl's forty-five-year-old aunt, Zoe. Flights to and from Australia were not commonplace in the early 1960s, whereas ship travel was. On-board the ship from Sydney to London, Zoe repeatedly told her family that if she was to die in England, never to leave her 'buried under the cold snow. Bring me back to the warm Australian sun.'

At the Corbett Arms pub in Ogmore Vale one night, when Krys's parents and the Johnstons, with Zoe, shared an amiable evening, his mother and Zoe got to talking about life after death. 'I promise you I'll come back and let you know if survival goes on', Zoe told his mother, Helen. That prediction came sooner than anyone was to think. Six months' later a letter arrived from the Johnstons – Zoe had died of a cerebral haemorrhage at their Weston-super-Mare hotel.

Two months after this incident, Krys's parents were in bed one night at about 11 p.m. It was a quiet night, with no breeze or rain. All at once, both began to hear a faint crackling sound 'like a whip hitting against wood', they later said. This sound began to grow louder, seemingly to echo around the head of the bed, next to his parents. His father got up and went to the window to see whether the television antenna was loose, or to see if there was some explanation for this whip-like sound, which by then was becoming more intense.

Nothing seemed to be causing the noise, so his father investigated further. He checked the second bedroom across the landing, then went downstairs. All the lights were off – except the overhead light in the bathroom. He could hear running water, so he opened the bathroom door – water was pouring into the toilet bowl. As he watched, he saw the cistern handle then rise by itself. He returned to the bedroom and told his wife what he had seen. By now, the strange, whip-like sound was even louder. When Krys's mother said to his father, 'Could that be Zoe come back to let us know she has survived death?', the whip-like sound actually began to diminish, growing fainter and fainter, until it died away.

The incident never happened again, and there was no explanation as to why the toilet would flush by itself or the bathroom light come on unaided. At that time, the property had been modernised, and this strange experience could not be tied to 'malfunctioning' fixtures.

So what can we say about these types of incident? Recent reports suggest ghostly experiences allegedly do happen around running water. Could there be rational, innocent explanations of what happened to all of them at Alma Terrace? Possibly. Could these incidents be coincidences or the product of overheated imaginations? Possibly. Might they be real phenomena and not readily dismissed? Yes, until we know otherwise, they are.

Whatever the origins of unexplained phenomena, they deserve investigation because they have such a powerful impact on the psychologies of those individuals who experience them.

That Krys can still feel the overshadowing power of the experiences he had in Alma Terrace, forty years ago, is proof enough.

The Watchful Ghost, Unnamed Village, West of Swansea

In 1989, when she was nine years old, Victoria was in primary school and living with her parents, older brother and sister. As long as she could remember her family seemed to have experienced paranormal activity in the house they lived in – even following them when they moved.

It all started when Victoria was at school one day and was playing with the younger year group. She saw what looked like the end of a very long black cape go past the classroom window. As far as she knew she was the only one who saw it and, thinking she had been mistaken, did not mention it to anyone. She saw it a few more times but only at school. Then one day when she was walking down an old railway track she saw the 'black cape' again. Victoria was starting to get a bit scared now so she told her mother, who said not to worry about it, but she would keep an eye out for it.

As time went by Victoria started to forget about the black-cape incidents until one night when she was in her bedroom. She had a small black and white television on a chair by her bedroom door. The television had little knobs that had to be turned to get each channel and Victoria had been sitting in front of it for about five minutes struggling to find a channel, although she'd never had trouble finding a channel on it before. Victoria's brother came and stood in the doorway and started chatting to her. Victoria chatted back, not looking up from trying to find the channel on the television. When eventually Victoria did look up she suddenly saw, just behind her brother, a tall black figure. It had no face and was just completely black from head to foot. Victoria was terrified, went as white as a sheet and screamed at the top of her voice, scaring the 'living daylights' out of her brother. As she screamed the figure seemed to move away, going towards her sister's bedroom.

A few weeks passed and Victoria was having a sleepover at her house with a couple of friends. She and her friend Amy were sitting on her bed having a really good laugh, and her other friend, Nicola, was sitting at the bottom of the bed with her back to the open door, when the black figure appeared again in the doorway. Even though it had no face, Victoria knew it was looking at her. As she screamed the figure disappeared again. Not many people believed a nine-year-old girl was being haunted by a black figure, but fortunately her mother did, and suggested that the figure was trying to get Victoria's attention or was looking out for her. It didn't seem to want to hurt her, but Victoria still didn't like it either way.

After this, Victoria experienced even more unusual phenomena.

One night she had gone to bed and the rest of her family were downstairs. She got into bed and went to sleep with her door open. She woke up sometime later with the feeling that the end of her duvet was being lifted up to reveal her feet. Being frozen with fear, she lay very still. This was the type of trick her brother would have played on her, but she knew that she would have heard the floorboards creak if it had been him. The house they were living in dated back to the seventeenth century when it had been a public house and the floorboards were very creaky. All Victoria remembered after that was waking up the next day feeling very glad that it was the morning.

On her sixteenth birthday she had a friend staying over. That night, when she was in the bathroom, she heard her friend talking to someone. She left the bathroom and walked into her bedroom expecting to find one of her family members in there with her friend, but the only person in the room was her friend looking extremely shaken. When she had recovered she told Victoria that she had seen a dark figure walking out of the bathroom and across the landing. Thinking it was Victoria she started talking to her, but when she didn't walk into the bedroom she went out onto the landing only to find that she was still in the bathroom. After that night, whenever Victoria had a friend staying overnight they always saw the black figure if they were left alone. Maybe it was checking up on them.

When Victoria turned eighteen she was at a friend's house and one of their neighbours walked in. She and the neighbour got talking and he asked her where she was from. When she told him where she lived, he asked her if she had heard of the ghost that used to haunt that house and seemed to look after the children who were there before her family moved in. Although Victoria was relieved to hear that others knew of the black figure she did not admit to him that she had seen the ghost. He then told her that before the house was a public house it had been a monastery and that the black figure that haunted the house was a monk.

Eight years later Victoria invited a group of paranormal investigators, Spooks Paranormal, to her family's house as they were moving and they wanted to achieve closure before it was sold. The mediums picked up on no fewer than eleven spirits in the house. In the bedroom that had been Victoria's, one of the psychics straight away picked up the spirit of a monk who was called 'Father Francis', and he immediately went onto his knees and started to pray. By this point Victoria had left the room in tears. However, she was soon asked to return to the bedroom as 'Father Francis' needed Victoria to forgive him for frightening her. She went back into the bedroom and forgave the monk.

Whether there have been any further hauntings by 'Father Francis' or any of the other spirits allegedly residing in Victoria's old house, we don't know. All we can say is that if you have children and live in an old cottage somewhere in to the west of Swansea, don't be too concerned. Someone's looking over them …

The Aroma of a Loved One, Unknown Location, Swansea

In the immediate aftermath of the Second World War, as Swansea slowly began to recover from the devastation wreaked across the town, attention became focused upon the housing shortage caused by the recent conflict and new buildings began to appear.

It was during this post-war building boom that one girl's family was able to move from their prefabricated house, so typical in late 1940s to early 1950s Britain, to a brand new council-built house.

The family, being the first to live there, were able to wholly put their own stamp upon it. However, it would seem that it was not only the young girl and her parents who were making their presence felt in the new house.

In a home which had not seen so much as a twist of tobacco, the ten-year-old child was astonished one day to be aware of a strong smell of pipe smoke as she walked through the house. However, there was nobody in this young girl's family who smoked, and as far as she

Swansea Town Centre, c.1910.

The remains of Swansea Castle, contrasting against a backdrop of Swansea's modern buildings.

was aware, no visiting friends that did either. If this was the case, where could such a strong and distinctive smell of pipe smoke have come from? It was not just that the smell itself had apparently spontaneously manifested itself that made this event so curious to the young girl, but also that she was immediately put in mind of her own grandfather. He was a man given to using a particular type of tobacco in his pipe but he certainly could not have been in the house. He had passed away several years earlier, before the family had set foot in their present home. Many years passed since this experience, and during this time the girl never noticed any other unexplained smells in the house, not least of pipe smoke. But this is not the end of the girl's strange story.

Some fifteen years later, no longer the young girl of this first experience, she had married and bought a house some miles away from her childhood home in one of Swansea's developing suburbs. It was a short while after moving to this house that she was stopped in her tracks one day while walking up the staircase. There it was once more. In a house where no one smoked, the distinctive smell of her grandfather's tobacco.

More than thirty-five years have since passed and it would seem the presence of this familiar aroma has now ceased. Despite being only two very brief and passing moments, now many years in the past, the woman will never quite forget how this strange and yet somewhat comforting smell made her feel.

Many people report instances where they may suddenly notice an aroma that puts them in mind of a friend or family member that has long since passed away, but are very rarely afraid of it. For many of us, these small experiences comfort us and allow us to believe that those who we have loved may still be in our lives in some way, no matter how brief.

A Very Eerie Temporary Home, Bridgend

This is a story that happened about thirty years ago to a young couple from South Wales, when they were trying to sell their current house and move into a newly built home ready to start their new life together. We will call them Linda and Roy for the purpose of this story. They had sold their own home but the completion date for the new house had been delayed by a week, one of those awful and frustrating situations that so often occur to those moving house. They either had to lose the sale of their own property or find somewhere else to live for one week to enable them to complete their move as planned.

They chose the latter, and so Linda frantically rang around several private renting agencies, including the local council. They were hoping at best to be offered a caravan or similar, but to their great surprise they were offered a two-bedroom house in the Bridgend area. As there were just the two of them and their cat, this option seemed perfect, so they loaded up the van and moved their furniture in. Since they were only staying for a single week, they did not put any furniture upstairs in the rented house and decided to sleep downstairs. They put their bed up alongside a glass door which led into the stairwell. They could see very clearly through this door.

The previous owners had left a bed upstairs and Linda and Roy found it very difficult to stop their cat sleeping on this bed and clawing and pawing at the mattress; after all, when a cat wants to do something there is little us humans can do to stop it! They just could not move their cat from this room.

The bridge that gives Bridgend its name.

When they entered the house for the first time, Linda remembers feeling an intense sensation of hopelessness, and when she walked past the bottom of the stairs she felt an icy-cold blast running right through her body. She thought nothing more of this and put her mood and feelings down to the stress of moving house, which at the time seemed a perfectly logical thing to do.

That first night, when the couple lay in bed, Linda just could not help looking through the glass door towards the bottom of the stairs, and suddenly out of the corner of her eye she was convinced she saw something that looked exactly like the shape of a man standing just on the other side of the door. When she then looked away and turned back, it was gone but a feeling of hopelessness and despair came flooding over her. She was sure that she had seen something through the door but all was now very quiet and still. She had seen the man standing at the foot of the stairs – but he was about 3ft in the air, as if he was suspended. As you can imagine, Linda did not get very much sleep that night, and when she did sleep her dreams were full of visions of someone else in the house with them. The night to her seemed endless.

The next day she went to work as usual, although very tired, and her husband stayed home to sort out some of the moving business. When he was leaving the house around lunchtime the next door neighbour introduced herself. When she had been chatting to Roy for about five minutes, she dropped into the conversation the bombshell that changed everything. Their neighbour had said, 'Of course, we never thought we would have neighbours for a long time after the previous tenant had hung himself from the top of the stairs after his wife had left him. Apparently he was there for six days!'

When Linda got home Roy told her the tale, and in a very short space of time they had packed a bag and left to stay with relatives, leaving all of their other belongings behind with the intention to come back for them another day, though this time in daylight. They dragged the cat from the bed upstairs, only to find out later that this was where the man had been laid out after he had been found in the stairwell.

Linda says she cannot explain the feelings she had in that house – only that she felt that something bad had happened and, combined with the feeling of being really cold at the bottom of the stairs, she felt very uneasy. The couple did not know the history of the house before they moved in, but Linda is still convinced today that the man she saw suspended in the air was the poor man who had taken his own life following a broken heart.

They moved their furniture out of the house the next day and asked friends to help them as they did not feel comfortable being there alone. They moved into their new house a week later, but never forgot their one night in the house in Bridgend, for it was certainly a memorable experience.

A Family Home, Pontarddulais

Pontarddulais used to be a thriving industrial community. It could boast a number of tinplate works, a busy railway junction and a coal mine. Before then it was a quiet, inconsequential little place, with its only importance being that it was here that people crossed the Loughar River. But it was the Rebecca Riots that brought rural Pontarddulais to prominence and more widely known to the world. Where the workingmen's club now stands was the site of the attack on the Pontarddulais Gate in September 1843 by a Rebecca leader called John Hughes. Unfortunately for him, he and his followers were apprehended by the authorities who were lying in wait. John Hughes was sentenced to twenty years' transportation to Tasmania, but never returned. It is said that Rebecca had visited earlier that year when the Bolgoed Gate was destroyed by Daniel Lewis, who still lies buried in the cemetery of Gopa Chapel. Because of these two attacks, the small hamlet of Pontarddulais grew in notoriety.

This story concerns a small bungalow, built nearly 100 years after these riots, on the outskirts of Pontarddulais.

Ainsley Page's grandparents moved to their bungalow in 1961. It was built in 1936 and five different families had lived there previously. Since the very beginning, Ainsley's grandparents reported having experienced unexplained phenomena in their home. The grandfather passed away nineteen years ago when Ainsley was a young girl, but because the paranormal activity has been occurring since 1961, the family did not believe it was connected to his death.

Ainsley's grandmother indicates that she is quite used to the presence in the home. She describes it as feeling quite friendly and she is more than happy to share some of her experiences with us. However, it is worth noting that Ainsley has always felt uneasy in the bungalow and she doesn't feel comfortable staying there for very long …

Ainsley's grandmother, alone at home in the lounge one day, heard strange scraping noises coming from the kitchen. Thinking that it might be some kind of animal, she investigated.

The centre of Pontarddulais.

War memorial in Pontarddulais.

Upon entering the kitchen she discovered that a decorative magnet had been moved across the fridge door in such a forceful manner that the white plastic had been damaged, revealing the metal underneath. As you can imagine, she was more than slightly annoyed!

One breakfast time, Ainsley's grandmother had made herself a slice of toast. As usual, she cut it in half. She ate one piece and then heard the doorbell. Leaving the other uneaten half on the plate, she went to the door to receive her mail from the postman. When she returned to eat the remains of her breakfast it had completely disappeared. She searched on the floor, under the table, on her clothes but it was nowhere to be seen. Later when she went into the pantry to get something, she found the missing slice of toast hidden behind a tin of food. There is no gap between the door and the pantry itself and it is always kept shut, so how did it manage to get there?

After having a bath, Ainsley's grandmother normally cleans the tub, and replaces a stool that she uses during bathing back across the bath. On one occasion, she heard the sound of scraping along the bath, and on inspection she discovered that the stool had been moved to the other end of the bath.

Living alone at home, Ainsley's grandmother would often travel to the bathroom during the night without turning a light on. On one occasion she got up in the night to go to the bathroom and as she passed the glass door that leads to the lounge, she noticed that there was a strange light on the wall. Earlier that evening she had pulled the curtains closed while watching the television, so she knew there was no light coming in from outside. As she stood there she watched as the light move up the wall, across the ceiling and headed into the central lampshade. The ceiling light then flickered. She opened the door carefully, and checked the light switch just inside the room. It was completely off.

Although Ainsley is unnerved by the place, her grandmother says that she is not really that bothered by what goes on, mainly because she is used to it. She claims that she does not know who it is, but occasionally when the activity gets on her nerves, she has been known to shout out, 'Just leave me alone!' Whether the residing spirit listens or not, we do not know!

A Neath Valley Haunting, Neath Valley

In the Neath Valley is a former farmhouse and outbuildings that were converted some years ago into a family home and office from where the present owners run their business. This family have lived with at least seven ghosts for the last ten years. To be fair the visiting spirits gave them time to settle in before they started. Then, one night, an elderly woman in a dressing gown appeared by the owner's bed in the early hours of the morning looking at him in an utterly disapproving manner. The apparition did this every night for a week, until the lady of the house got fed up and sought the advice of a local medium. The psychic suggested that she should confront the spectre and tell it that one should not wake people up at night as it was not the polite thing to do. Surprisingly this challenge had the desired effect and this particular apparition was never seen again.

A few weeks later a new activity started in the outbuilding that contained the utility room and the central-heating boiler along with its control panel. The first they knew that anything was wrong was when the central heating went off one cold winter's night. As her husband was

An eastern view of the Neath Valley.

away on business his wife put on some warm clothes and went down to check the boiler. She soon found that the control panel had been switched off and, after resetting all the controls, returned to bed. A few days later the same thing happened again, so in the morning she called the heating engineer out, thinking that some electrical fault was causing the problem. The engineer checked out the system, but could find no faults at all. The next event again seemed to be a fault as the timing devices seemed to be malfunctioning with the zoned heating coming on and turning off at times which had not been programmed. This time the husband went into the utility room and arrived just in time to see unseen hands turning the dials back and forth. So they now had a mischievous entity playing tricks on them. They decided to take the same course of action as before and tell the invisible culprit that it was not funny and to leave everything alone. They were now getting quite used to their resident ghosts and began to enjoy the challenge.

They were unaware that anybody else was privy to their unseen visitors to the property until they tried to get some work done on the house. They decided the floorboards needed sanding as their youngest daughter had received a nasty splinter in her knee from playing on the bedroom floor. They obtained the name of the contractor who did the original carpentry and woodwork during the renovation; however, he said that they were booked up for months. They soon found that all the local firms who could do the job made excuses or just did not come back. Eventually they hired a sander and did the job themselves, and all that was left was to hire the services of a decorator to repaint the room and varnish the floor. This contractor was only too willing to do the job and a week later he arrived, and the family soon found out why. On his first day he told them that he was fascinated by ghosts and had always wanted to

A northern view of the Neath Valley.

work in a haunted house. When asked how he knew the house was haunted, he came up with the following story that was well known amongst the local builders.

During the renovation, a carpenter and his mate had been carrying out the final trimming of the extensive new woodwork. Unbeknownst to the carpenter, his mate had just gone out to the van to fetch some more tools when heavy footsteps crossed the recently boarded floor above him. He went to the stairwell and shouted up to tell his mate to stop messing about and bring him the tool he needed. It was then that his work colleague came through the front door. After telling his mate what he had just heard, the pair ascended the stairs only to find the upstairs room empty, and in fact a short inspection of the buildings soon revealed they were the only ones on the site. The next day, both of them were sitting on the stairs, eating their sandwiches, when a loud crash was heard from the same bedroom and again there was no obvious cause. Two days later there were two events that resulted in these workmen leaving the site for good. The pair both heard the now familiar thuds and footsteps, but this time they saw a dark shadow at the top of the stairs. They picked up the remainder of their tools and made for the door, pelted by the odd nail thrown by an invisible hand. Needless to say the story soon spread amongst local builders and probably resulted in the current reluctance of many local contractors to work there.

Far from being frightened by this story the occupants looked forward to further paranormal activity developing. They did not have to wait long, as soon the entity they nicknamed 'The Grumpy Farmer' began to make its presence felt. At first it was small ornaments that appeared to have mysteriously moved, then small items of furniture. It appeared that if it really did not like anything it disappeared and was eventually found somewhere outside. Their daughter actually named the culprit as she said that the place always smelt of farmyard manure when anything had mysteriously been moved. As this activity continued the family began to have second thoughts about the sex of this entity. It soon became obvious that the clothes of the male members of the family or visitors were the next targets. Men's clothes put tidily away in drawers or wardrobes would be found strewn across the bedrooms by unseen hands. Curiously, women always felt very comfortable in the house and their clothes were never touched. The changing nature of these activities puzzled the occupants and they decided that perhaps one or more of their invisible visitors got bored and thus frequently rang the changes in their activities. Alternatively they thought it could be different entities coming and going that resulted in the variety of activity and phenomena.

Out of all the paranormal activity at this house, the next one was the only one to concern them. They had installed a cat flap in the kitchen door to allow their three cats to come and go as they pleased. Late one night the eldest daughter was making a hot drink before retiring, when the youngest cat came crashing through the flap and this was followed by a loud bang on the door. Unusually the cat had turned towards the door and began hissing at the door with its hackles rising as an even louder bang shook the door. Terrified, the girl woke her parents, fearing an intruder was trying to break into the property. On the way downstairs they all heard another series of thuds against the kitchen door. When the three of them arrived in the kitchen, two of the cats were now facing the door, both in a defensive mode. Reluctant to open the door the husband moved to a window where he could clearly see outside the door and the yard beyond. There was nothing out there, so after five minutes, he dressed, got a torch and went out to investigate armed with a walking stick, whilst his wife held the mobile telephone ready to phone the police. A comprehensive inspection of the immediate surroundings revealed nothing visible, but he did feel very cold at one point and constantly had the feeling that something was watching him. Before locking up he secured the cat flap and then they retired. If this was an intruder then why make so much noise to alert the residents? Perhaps it was a large wild animal of some sort or a stray dog after the cat. If it was supernatural then maybe a not-so-friendly entity had entered the frame.

As far as we are aware the family are still experiencing what they call benign activity, although the frequency has decreased considerably. Have these ghosts grown bored with haunting this property in the Vale of Neath and moved on?

The Caewathan Estate, Skewen

By the age of eight, Brady had already lived at five addresses in the Neath area. Then his father was made redundant and he and his family made their last change of home as a 'birth family unit'. Brady and his family were lucky and were allocated a council house on the Caewathan Estate in Skewen – a semi-detached property with a view of Skewen Park.

Skewen, a pretty village in the county of Neath Port Talbot, was once an industrial village. There were a number of collieries surrounding the village – The Crown and Mines Royal Copper Works and the Cheadle and Neath Abbey Ironworks were once important industrial sites which stood close by. Also very close by are the fantastic ruins of Neath Abbey, an amazing and atmospheric location originally founded by Richard De Granville in 1130. Neath Abbey

Skewen High Street.

remains to this day one of the most fascinating historic monuments in Wales, and is without doubt worth visiting.

On moving to their new house in Skewen, the family discovered that the previous tenant had died with no traceable family and had left various personal effects in the house, items that Brady's mother soon got rid of. Brady is convinced that it is because of the items she removed that the experiences began.

Brady was considered 'artistic' as a child and was allowed to paint murals on the walls of his bedroom. His black dragon rising up on a flame orange wall would often draw stares from passengers sitting on the top deck of the 153 bus. However, one fit of youthful exuberance saw Brady paint the panels on the exterior of his bedroom door in oils. Then, in an effort to stall the family's complaints, he attempted to cover his efforts with a metallic silver paint. Brady puts this down to him being young, and it was the seventies after all!

As a punishment, and after his mother had stopped screaming, Brady's door was removed and he had to sleep facing out onto the landing. It was shortly after this episode that he realised something very strange was going on. He started to notice that their bathroom door, opposite his room on the landing, was slowly opening and shutting of its own accord. Brady reported this strange occurrence rather excitedly to his parents, only to be told off for talking rubbish and trying to frighten his younger sister. For years the door would swing quietly open and shut at night until he became quite blasé about it.

Things turned a little more serious when Brady was eleven. He was home recovering from surgery one day when someone started to walk quite loudly up the stairs. The footsteps never reached the top and he could not get anyone to respond to his calling out. Over the years, both his sister and father also reported the sound of footsteps climbing the stairs. At one time his

The old stone bridge in Skewen.

father, who was ill in bed, called them all 'rotten' because one of the family had come quietly up the stairs, watched him for a while over the top of the staircase, and then gone back down without going in to see him in the bedroom. However, at the time this was meant to have taken place, the whole family could confirm that it was not any of them.

Around this time Brady, was considered old enough to look after his sister if his parents popped out to the pub in the evening. They would watch television together whilst their mother joined their father for an hour or so. Brady and his sister would just sit there, not daring to go into the hallway, not even to the toilet. They would very often just wait in the one room until an adult returned. Brady remembers one particular night when they did venture out into the hall when there were no adults present. He vividly remembers his sister, while facing him, suddenly going very pale and starting to point behind him, stammering, not being able to speak. Brady refused to turn around, even though the family dogs were watching and growling at something too. His sister later told him that a woman had walked through the door to the hall, stopped to stare at Brady from behind for a while, then passed through the outer wall.

Another occurrence some time later took place one afternoon after Brady had been spending time with his friends in the park opposite his house. He remembers sitting in the park as his friends were about to start heading home. When they asked why Brady wasn't heading back to his own house, he replied, 'Look at the curtains in my house'. The friends, gazing up at the house, noted the curtains upstairs were opening and closing. Brady then calmly explained that his parents and sister had gone shopping and there was no one at home.

Some years later Brady joined the Air Force and only ever returned to the house when on leave.

As a last comment, Brady added that one time his fiancée came to stay in the house with him for the weekend. She went into the hall one evening to get the vacuum cleaner, only to come running back to say there was something with red eyes in the hall! And it was watching her…

Brady often passes the house and wonders if other tenants have had the same experiences as they did. But as Brady says: 'It doesn't seem fair to ask.'

The Aberavon Bwgan, Aberavon

The old Welsh word 'Bwgan' was used to describe an entity that was both mischievous and at the same time threatening. It is believed that the word has the same root as the Irish and Scottish word 'Bogle', describing a hobgoblin, bugbear or poltergeist. It has also been proposed that the English phrase 'Bogey Man' also evolved from such roots. Could it be then that the area now known as Baglan was a corruption of this Welsh word and referred to a place where frequent paranormal activity took place in ancient times?

Alongside Baglan is the Aberavon area of Port Talbot, which has, according to historical sources, occupied at least three different locations due to the changing nature of the coastline down the centuries. It is believed that the first two settlements were situated nearer to the sea, but there are no visible signs now to show where. When they were constructing the nearby dock in the 1830s, a variety of ancient artefacts were unearthed. These finds ranged from Roman through to medieval, and indicate that there had been settlements at these sites for some considerable time. The Aberavon that can be seen today started in the mid-nineteenth century and was considerably augmented in the mid-twentieth century with the building of

Aberavon beach in the early evening.

the large Sandfields housing estate and the construction of a formalised promenade and the Lido. This tale comes from this new part of the town and concerns an incident that happened in the recent past.

One day, neighbours were surprised to see a family vacating their council house, especially as they had only occupied it for less than twelve months. Much speculation passed between the locals, as once you had obtained a house in those days you were loath to give it up without good reason. With that in mind, and the added difficulty of finding temporary accommodation for both themselves and their young children, speculation was rife as to what had made them so adamant never to spend another night in what had become their home. Recently the full story behind this incident came out and their reasons for leaving the house became clear.

Events began with simple unexplained phenomena and escalated to more serious events. The family were first aware of the lights in various rooms being switched off as though by an unseen hand. Thinking it was an electrical fault they asked an electrician friend to check over the wiring and switches. He found that everything was in order and detected no faults in either the system or the switches. The husband worked on shifts at the local steel works and therefore his wife and two children were often left alone in the house at night. The wife was awoken on one of these nights by the duvet apparently being pulled from her bed. She ignored it the first time, attributing some logical explanation to the occurrence. Some weeks passed and again when her husband was at work some unseen force seemed to pull the duvet of her while she slept. A few days later the parents were both awakened by screaming coming from their five-year-old daughter's bedroom. Rushing into the room they found their daughter sitting up in bed with all her clothes and a beanbag piled onto her bedclothes.

They moved their daughter in with them after the incident and things quietened down over the next few weeks with no further activity from these unseen forces. Then again the parents were awakened by their daughter's screams from her bedroom that she had only just returned to. This time the bed was untouched, but their daughter pleaded with them to stop whoever was banging her head and pulling her hair. Once again they comforted their daughter and moved her in with them. The pair discussed the events and put it down to a bad dream brought on by the previous incident and let her stay back with them. However, events were soon to take a more serious turn a few days later. The mother was entering the front room when she suddenly saw a book being propelled towards her at great speed. Luckily she just had time to shut the door and the book hit the closing door with a bang, thus saving her from possible injury. Cautiously she opened the door, picked up the book and was horrified to see that it was a Bible that had been in the bookcase on the far wall. The next event happened in the kitchen when the mother was cooking dinner. She had put a stew and the vegetables on to cook, when some fifteen minutes later she heard a rap on the front door. Opening the door she found no one in sight and decided that either the impatient caller had left or the local children were playing games. It was then that she noticed the unpleasant smell of burning food and ran back into the kitchen. The sight that greeted her there was upsetting to say the least, with all the food spread across the kitchen floor. What was more frightening was the fact that the pans remained on the cooker almost empty and now burning dry.

In view of the implications and dangers caused by these latest incidents, the family decided to seek professional help in this matter and contacted an expert in the field. She duly visited the premises and claimed to have cleared the troublesome entity. Things were certainly better over the next few weeks. However, this situation was only a brief respite and more was yet to come. The family returned from shopping one day to find cut flowers, as well as the water they were in, strewn liberally around the house. It was at this point that the family made the decision to leave their home come what may. Perhaps as a triumphant gesture the entity had one more surprise up its sleeve for the man of the house. Returning from a nightshift in the early morning he opened the door to be faced with a dark swirling shadow in the hall that dissipated as he ran towards it. The family packed up what they needed and left the house later that day. Was this the work of infamous Bwgan, or is there a more rational explanation for the phenomena?

Five

Spirits of the Great Outdoors

People have long associated ghosts with old buildings and castles, but the unexplained phenomena in our world is by no means restricted to being indoors. Many a person out for a quiet walk in the countryside, a ramble through town, or a drive under cover of night, has stumbled upon a sight or experience that has left them, at best, perplexed!

The outdoors in Wales is a place that many people spend their leisure time, which is no surprise when you consider that the Gower coast to the south of Swansea is often thought of as being one of the most beautiful places to visit in the whole of the United Kingdom.

In this chapter we would like to introduce you to a series of chilling tales from the great outdoors, beginning with one recounted by historian and paranormal enthusiast, Lesley Smith.

Pembrey Woods, Pembrey

In 2007 SWPR invited renowned Tutbury Castle historian and *Most Haunted* regular, Lesley Smith, to become their third patron (to work alongside local historian Val Williams and well-known American author and parapsychologist Loyd Auerbach). SWPR has a strong interest in preserving and promoting Welsh history and heritage, and as such thought that Lesley Smith would make the ideal addition to the team. After research into SWPR and the work they do, Lesley Smith agreed, and has since become a very active and enthusiastic patron.

The following account is direct from Lesley Smith. She talks about her visit to Pembrey Woods, one of the locations for Living TV's *Most Haunted* in their tenth season:

Pembrey Country Park.

Pembrey Woods is rather a surprise for those who do not know the area well. Despite 'The Live' being held in Llanelli a couple of years ago I did not have the chance in a hectic filming schedule to explore more than the sites the show would come from.

A beautiful cream beach in a soft pink sunset was the last view I expected as we left the rather industrial urban basin. However, as the light dropped, the woods just off the beach took on a very different atmosphere. Of course, it is important to take a grip on rising fear, and even panic, when faced with a strange area and light dropping. It is an animal instinct to be cautious and watchful. I am aware of this and pushed fear deep down inside of me, concentrating on the history instead.

The waters around the beach are lethal. Dozens of ships were lost and thousands of lives as well as valuable cargoes ranging from wool to, some say, slaves.

It is said that when a ship floundered and tipped, locals came in large numbers for a well-practiced salvage operation. Some souls washed upon the shores alive were dispatched by having their heads beaten in, whilst others had fingers or parts of limbs removed to take off rings or bracelets, arguing no doubt that 'you can't take it with you'. However, stealing from the dead is a crime that raises revulsion for these vultures as much now as it did then. The great worry was that some of these corpses were not corpses when they arrived on the beach but dazed and shocked by the wrecking of their ship only to find no mercy. It would not be difficult to kill someone in those circumstances – just leave them lying on the shore in a cold wind and in minutes hyperthermia would take the most hardy having just left cold waters. No mercy indeed.

A view into the woods at Pembrey.

A very old hotel in Pembrey.

The woods, so pretty in the daylight became black and sinister in the moonlight. Suddenly I was aware of a low whistle. Not any animal or bird I had ever heard before, and then another from a different place, as if in answer, and then another, quickly followed by a movement in the bracken between the trees. Suddenly it felt as if we were surrounded by people dipping low like animals, creeping around us. They were known, when alive, as 'the men with little hatchets' - the hatchets were used to smash into and lever off the lids from sea chests. As I stood frozen still with other members of the team I was aware that I was not the only one that felt as if we were surrounded.

Then a light appeared – low and flickering in the woods a lantern lit with a candle rather than a bright modern battery light from a car or torch. I am very used to candlelit lanterns in my castle so the look of it is familiar to me. The ground started to rustle and creep around us as if we were being surrounded and I had to fight rising panic. It could have been animals, the candlelight may have been a faulty battery and the sense of being surrounded and dark movements in the trees could have been imagination born of a little too much knowledge of the history of the area. Then again it might not have been …

Echoes of Air Raids, Swansea Town Centre

Being an important seaport at the outbreak of the Second World War, the town of Swansea and its docks had more than its fair share of air raids with the resultant loss of life and destruction. By far the worst bombing occurred in what was called 'The Three Nights Blitz' on 19, 20 and 21 February 1941. Contemporary records show that these raids lasted a total of over thirteen hours, resulting in severe damage to the docks and the almost total obliteration of old Swansea town centre. It is believed that these raids led to 230 deaths and almost 400 casualties. Such trauma and emotional outpouring must have had an effect on the energies of the area.

No wonder then that workers over the years since, in both the docks and adjacent factories, have reported blood-curdling screaming and the dull thuds of explosions, together with the smell of burning oil. However, it was in the now city centre that perhaps one of the most dramatic sightings has been experienced. Whilst working for a well-known security company, one of their employees came out with this spine-chilling story of an apparition he saw one night in the city centre. The relief guard had been late coming on duty, due to family problems, and this resulted in our man leaving the premises in the early hours of the morning. As he walked to his car he saw the outline of someone staggering towards him. Assuming that he was a drunk he gave the oncoming figure a wide berth and avoided making eye contact. An icy blast suddenly hit him and he turned to see a man dressed in what he described as a British airman's uniform of the 1940s vintage and the man appeared to have horrific injuries.

The security guard said that he suddenly realised it was a ghost and ran off. It was some years later that he revealed the incident, and then only in the company of someone who would believe him. It is possible that an airman lost his life when spending some leave in the town, only to be the victim of an air raid. However, some years later a much more interesting story was told about what happened in the area of the apparition. Records show that three uniformed members of the RAF joined locals in an air-raid shelter located in the very centre of town. As the intensity of the air raid increased, all three airmen decided to leave the shelter to see if

St Mary's Church, Swansea town centre.

they could assist with fire-fighting and rescue duties in the immediate vicinity. Just outside the shelter, one of the airmen is reported to have spotted an incendiary bomb and tried to cover it with a sandbag, when it suddenly and unexpectedly exploded. Sadly, this brave airman soon died of his injuries. As far as it can be made out, the sighting of the apparition and the location of this incident correlate pretty well. Was then the trauma of this incident etched upon the very ether of this part of the modern city forever?

Another victim of the Second World War has paranormal as well as folklore connotations, although not in the same way as the last tragedy. We must first go back to the late nineteenth century, when the parish church of St Mary underwent a much-needed restoration. At that time the contract was awarded to a prominent architect, much to the displeasure of another bidder. It is said that this other architect was so incensed that he bought the land and built a folly opposite the refurbished church in order to house a wooden statue of the devil. It was said that he was delighted that his statue's evil eyes would forever gaze on the church. Folklore says that he also had a curse put upon the statue along the lines: 'My devil will be able to leer and laugh, for at some time in the future he will see St Mary's burn to the ground.'

Call it coincidence or something else, his curse came to fruition when, during an air raid in February 1941, St Mary's Church and most of Swansea's centre was razed to the ground by incendiary bombs. People were amazed to see that the wooden statue of the devil and his watchtower were one of the few artefacts left standing in the whole area. In the 1950s and 1960s an extensive programme of building took place in order to restore the war-damaged centre. St Mary's was deemed a priority and 'The Swansea Devil', or 'Old Nick' as it was now called, was once more watching the object of his hex rebuilt. Finally, in 1962, the statue was

'Old Nick' overlooking St Mary's Church in his new home.

removed (some say on purpose) in order that the now unsafe purpose-built watchtower could be demolished. Around this time the statue mysteriously disappeared for many years, until a local historian managed to trace its location to a garage in Gloucester. The historian returned the 'devil' back to Swansea to continue his watch over St Mary's. As his old watchtower had long gone and was now replaced by the Quadrant Centre, permission was gained to install Swansea's most curious artefact within the centre's Whitewall entrance.

Whether you love or hate it probably depends on your religious views and what you believe the statue represents. Experts today are still baffled as to how the statue survived the firestorm that destroyed everything else made of wood around it. Despite all the odds, the 'Swansea Devil' seems to have a supernatural knack of always returning to its original position and the task given to it by that long dead architect. Some people believe that inanimate objects can have, or may take on, an entity of their own – perhaps one possible explanation for Swansea's Old Nick?

Parc le Breos Scout Camp, Parkmill

The following incident happened to a member of the support staff for a Cub Scout camp on the Gower at Parkmill almost thirty years ago. Two of the camp staff would take turns to stay up each night in order to cover any emergency and generally ensure the site's security. After the usual problems of the first few nights away from home with some of their charges and the general ability of children of that age to try and stay up all night, things settled down. It was therefore later in the week, in order to punctuate the boredom of their vigil, that they took turns to indulge in short walks from the campsite. It was during one of these walks that one experienced a new aspect of the unexplained.

The village of Parkmill lies just west of Swansea, on the Gower, and is perhaps best known for its twelfth-century water-powered corn and saw mill that is now a heritage centre. The mill itself has been the focus of much paranormal activity in recent years, although in those days it was just a collection of buildings with an air of dereliction. They were camped at the campsite half a mile further up the valley, known locally as Cwm Gwyrdd. This valley is one of the hidden jewels of the Gower, and was, with the mill, part of the medieval deer park of the local Norman de Breos family.

The limestone caves that lurk unseen in the woods that border this valley had evocative names like Tooth and Cat Hole, and contained artefacts that suggested that these caves were first occupied in the Upper Palaeolithic period, probably used as a transit camp when our earliest ancestors were following the animals in the Ice Age. However, it is the restored remains of a so-called burial chamber of the Neolithic period of history that makes this one of those special places in the landscape. Not a lot is known about the prehistoric tribes that built this edifice and erected many other megaliths across the Gower, but quite a bit is known about the Lord William de Breos. According to chroniclers of the time, he was a nasty piece of work and did not care much for the local Welsh inhabitants. It is recorded that he imprisoned and slew many of them and replaced them with farmers he had shipped over the Bristol Channel from North Devon and Somerset. Stories abound on how he used the caves to imprison and torture the former inhabitants of the area, and there are rumours that he used to hunt his captives in the park, as he rated them more expendable than his precious deer. This now quiet and tranquil

Campsite at Parkmill.

valley must have seen its fair share of death and trauma in the past and, as with every other place, this leaves an unseen impression on the very ether. It is against this historical background that the story unfolds.

It was a clear starlit night with almost a full moon as one of the support staff headed from the campsite up the track that snakes its way along the valley. It was warm with just the hint of a breeze coming from a seaward direction and carrying the faint smell of brine with it. As he approached the burial chamber he began to see a swirling mist forming along the centre of the valley. This in itself was not unusual, as he had seen such effects many times before as the early morning dew formed on the grass. The idea came into his head that this unfolding scene would make a good location for a horror movie. It was then that the faint sounds of drumming, voices and singing or chanting drifted across the air towards him from further up the valley. Expecting to find the source of the sounds, he walked up the track to the deserted house at the end and then back to the chamber. There was no one there but him, and yet the sounds of people and music seemed to follow him at the same level wherever he went.

His search continued for about twenty minutes, at which point the sounds stopped and coincidentally the mist started to dissipate. He walked back to the campsite and was, to say the least, puzzled by the experience. It would have been nice to say that he had seen the ghosts of ancient Britons or a medieval lord and his entourage, but there was nothing. A nice moonlight view of Parc le Breos, the burial chamber and a strange swirling mist was all he had seen, and yet there were these sounds from an unknown source. The years went by and he visited this site many times, yet he was unable to catch the almost magical atmosphere and sounds of that night. However, as his experience of both the paranormal and unseen energies expanded, he looked deeper for the possible causes for the experience.

The burial chamber at Parkmill.

Parc le Breos limekiln.

The valley is both surrounded and crossed by many underground watercourses rushing through fissures and caves in the local rock formations. This creates very energetic water and there is strong evidence that our ancient ancestors often placed their megalithic structures at intersections of such unseen waterways, perhaps to harness energy for some unknown purpose. Paranormal research has also shown that unseen entities also seem to be attracted to comparable sources of energy, and apparitions often appear in similar locations. Sound is just another type of energy vibration, so is it therefore possible for sounds of a bygone age to be stored and recovered on demand by some process we do not yet fully understand? Can human emotions and even an imprint of our very being also be recorded on these energy fields? From its known history, this site has experienced its fair share of trauma and celebration as well as the unknown religious rites of the ancients. As has already been said, there has been a lot of paranormal activity in recent years around the mill. In addition, there is an old folk tale about the area that has some interesting connotations.

The tale goes that a young woman would go into Park Woods for a secret assignation with a handsome young man. Her friends in the village became suspicious, as when questioned she did not seem to know much about the man or where he lived. It was agreed amongst her friends that one would secretly follow her on one of her mysterious trips. From her hiding place, the friend observed the young woman talking to an invisible suitor. The story goes that the friend alerted her to the fact that she was being beguiled by a demon, at which point an invisible force picked up a large rock and hurled it at the pair, but luckily it landed in the stream. Today, of course, we would recognise that the legend probably evolved from a woman who was a psychic and was communicating with a spirit entity, showing that this area has been a spiritually active location for some considerable time.

The Bishopston Hauntings, Bishopston

The unexplained knows no boundaries, and the border between folklore and the paranormal is often blurred. This is particularly true in Wales. The haunting of the former rectory at Bishopston is a case to prove the point. The story goes that an elderly cleric once occupied the rectory, and had lived there alone since the death of his wife. He started to appear drawn and haggard, and when asked by his parishioners if everything was all right, he came out with this strange tale. He confessed that he had not been able to eat and sleep properly for several months due to the regular appearance of an apparition of an old woman dressed in white. Being a man of God, he began to suspect that this was some divine retribution for some sin he had unknowingly committed. Over the months the spectre had changed from a faint light being in a swirling mist to something much more substantial and threatening. Just before he told others about his experiences, her features had begun to materialise, and her eyes burning like the fires of hell particularly terrified him. Later, another feature accompanied the appearances: the low sound of a beating heart. As the weeks went on the volume of the heartbeat increased and soon the resultant vibrations began to effect crockery and furniture in the rectory.

Following his revelations it is said that many fellow clergy and other people visited the rectory in order to see the haunting by the White Lady. Unfortunately, the spectre would not

Bishopston seafront, looking down the Gower Peninsula.

appear to any of them. Inevitably the parishioners suspected that their rector was suffering from senile dementia and petitioned the Bishop to have him removed. Help came from an unlikely source, as it is said a gypsy woman selling 'Lucky Heather' called one day at the rectory. The rector opened the door and the gypsy looked behind him and shrieked, 'A ghost, a ghost!'

The cleric, aware of the reputation of the Romany folk for their knowledge of the supernatural, eventually managed to persuade her to help him rid the rectory of the unwelcome visitor. The gypsy outlined a service of exorcism that would be successful in clearing this type of ghost. The woman insisted that her instructions be carried out exactly as she had described them with no deviations. Twelve men were first brought to the rectory and seated around a table on which stood twelve bells and the same number of lighted candles. They awaited the clock striking the first hour of midnight, for the gypsy had said that the ghost had an affinity with the dark side and it would attempt to extinguish the candles. She added that if the ghost extinguished every candle before the last stroke of midnight the exorcism would fail. If each man rang the bell in front of him and the rector read the Christian exorcism rite out aloud, the unwelcome spirit would be forced to leave the rectory forever.

As midnight approached, a growing sense of unease and silence descended amongst those gathered in the rectory. Unlike on other occasions, the spectre of the White Lady appeared on cue accompanied by the thundering heartbeat, and it is reported that the furniture around the group began to shake. Despite their fear, each man was determined to play their part in the unfolding drama. The ghost headed straight for the table to snuff out the candles, extinguishing the first one easily. The men now sounded their hand bells and the rector began to read from

Another view of the Bishopston seafront.

the service book. Immediately the White Lady became disorientated and confused, just as the gypsy woman had promised. When the clock had struck for the last time the White Lady is said to have left the rectory forever.

Another example of the overlap of folklore and the paranormal is the reported paranormal activity in the ancient sunken lane that goes from the village of Bishopston down to the sea at a point called The Knap. Trails of ghostly lights are often seen descending the lane in a procession towards the sea. Local legend has it that if one is foolhardy enough to follow them you will be led into a labyrinth of paths in the woods from which it is very difficult to find the way out. Some say that the lights are warriors returning to the Iron Age fort that lies by a bend in the river, whilst others claim they are miners going to work in the lead and silver mines that have been worked since Roman times which lie between the Knap and Caswell. Some others believe that it is the ghosts of smugglers or wreckers moving their ill-gotten goods from the beach to the village. Sceptics put this phenomenon down to ignited marsh gas formed by the damp nature of the lane and the decomposing plant material in it. What is certain is that it is sometimes difficult to find the way in these woods even in broad daylight, as though being led astray by an unseen hand. In the centre of Caswell Bay, close to the point where the river meets the sea, it is possible to witness a strange movement in the sand and to hear curious whispers or even the murmur of a heartbeat. Local folklore says that this is the White Lady who now undertakes the impossible task set by the rector and his men that day, to build a sandcastle capable of withstanding the tide's ebb and flow. Perhaps it is also her ghostly image trying to find the way back to a rectory that is no longer there?

The Wellington Bomber Crash Site, Carreg Goch

On a cold and windy day in February, Teresa took the long, hard hike to the top of a mountain called Carreg Goch. This is about 520m above Dan-yr-Ogof Showcaves in the Swansea Valley. She was making her way to the top of the mountain to see the legendary crash site of a Wellington bomber. Now a well-maintained war memorial, the site is a common target for seasoned walkers and every Remembrance Day a service is held there.

Teresa and her friend parked in a lay-by close to Craig y Nos Castle, where the famous opera singer Adelina Patti once lived, and they made their way up the steep hill. Although the weather was very cold, it was a bright and sunny day.

As they drew near to the crash site, Teresa's companion explained that he thought that they were within 200 yards of the wreckage, but it was difficult to find as it was hidden amongst the rocks. For some unknown reason, Teresa said she just knew which way to walk, and exclaimed excitedly, 'It's over that way', and pointed to her left. They walked over a little ridge and there to her complete surprise was the wreckage – right in front of them. It is still a mystery to her how she knew in which direction the plane was, as the wreckage was very well hidden, and the surrounding area quite vast.

By this point the temperature was around -10°C with the strong wind chill. Fortunately, as the pair had wrapped up well before heading out, they did not feel the cold too much.

Memorial plaque at the Wellington bomber crash site.

Teresa instantly had a feeling that this was a very desperate place. They approached the site and when she was about 20m away from the wreckage of the fuselage she felt a cold tingling along her spine. Even taking into account the wind chill, she was sure this icy feeling was not down to the cold. She described it as a 'different kind of cold. It made my spine tingle. I could not explain this feeling, but it made me feel sad.'

The wreckage of the bomber is strewn over quite a large area, but the bulk of the plane is in one place. There is a small memorial placed to the side of the wreckage and poppy wreaths are laid every Remembrance Sunday. This is a very poignant and sad place. Teresa once again felt the atmosphere was one of extreme despair, and believed that these thoughts were beginning to affect her.

At the site there is a book which names the deceased airmen, and also includes a brief life history of these poor men. It was while Teresa was reading this book that she suddenly felt incredibly unwell; the feeling in her stomach was indescribable. She also felt really sad and the fate of the airmen consumed her thoughts. She felt as though she were reliving their dreadful crash. She could sense the feeling of despair, absolute panic and fear. Looking around she noticed that although the wind was strong, the area around where she was standing was still and silent. Was she feeling the emotions of a young airman about to lose his life?

On 20 November 1944 this Wellington bomber crashed because the engine froze as they flew into an icy rain cloud, and on that bitterly cold night the plane lost power. Teresa felt very sad that if they had flown maybe 15m higher they would have cleared the top of the hill and lived. As she was feeling very unwell by now, they decided to make their way back to the car. As she moved away from the crash site she began to feel better and the feeling of panic began to subside.

Her companion told her that he has been at this site many times with people. He said that sometimes people were affected in the same way as Teresa had been, and sometimes the same people would feel nothing at all. Teresa stated that she had no prior knowledge of the way in which people had been affected. All she really knew was that some Canadian airmen had crashed into the mountain. So what was it that she had felt on that mountain top that day? In her own words Teresa said:

> Never before have I experienced feelings so intense, feelings that consumed my whole thoughts. I intend going back one day. It was a compelling place.

The B4281 from Aberkenfig, Bridgend

If you are travelling west from Bridgend to Swansea these days you will probably use the M4 or the A48, and you would probably never think of using the alternative B4281 from Aberkenfig to Kenfig Hill for that leg of the journey. Until relatively recent times this was just one leg of the main route used for such journeys. In common with many early Welsh roads it avoided the low-lying swampy areas by traversing the local high ground as much as possible. Some of the prehistoric standing stones that probably marked an even more ancient track now stand forgotten in fields along its way. This track would have seen its fair share of travellers going to the villages, towns and castles of Swansea and the Gower, as well as the monks travelling to

Margam Abbey. On a cold rainy winter's night the mist rolls across the road like the backdrop to a horror movie. It is not surprising then, that in such conditions the locals have given this stretch of road the nickname 'The Haunted Highway', and, as you will see, with good reason.

The first stories centre on residents of Pyle and Kenfig Hill, who are usually returning from a night out in Bridgend. One would suspect that at least some of these people were using this route to lessen the chance of being stopped by the police. The first tale comes from the mother of a motorcyclist and concerns an incident that happened to her son's girlfriend on their return from the cinema. It was late autumn and overcast, but not too cold, as they passed the junction at Fountain, and it was here that the motorcycle began to misfire; nevertheless, they managed to get it up to the top before it eventually expired. They pulled into a field gateway and the motorcyclist tried for about half an hour to restart it with no avail. He decided to walk back down the hill to the junction, as he knew there was a public phone box from where he could call for assistance. The girlfriend protested that she was too tired to walk back up the hill and so opted to stay with the bike. The motorcyclist then hurried down the hill to call for assistance.

He had only gone about 500 yards when he heard his girlfriend screaming from where he had just left her. He broke into a sprint and met his hysterical girlfriend coming just as fast towards him. It appears that after he had left she had lit up a cigarette and was leaning on the field gate looking into the gloom. At first she heard what she described as a low gruff voice from the hedge alongside, but after a cursory inspection failed to find anyone or indeed anything. She therefore put it down to imagination. It was then that what appeared to be an invisible icy hand firmly gripped hers. She panicked and the rest you know. Well, not quite, as the next day it is alleged that faint bruising began to appear on the hand of the girl in question. Luckily for them, that night a neighbour of the motorcyclist came by a short time later and took them both home.

The next incident is a phenomenon that has been reported by many people down the years at roughly the same spot on the outskirts of the village of Cefn Cribwr. A man who had just finished his late shift at the Ford plant in Bridgend was returning to his home in Kenfig Hill along the road. In his car headlights he caught the outline of a woman dressed in white crossing the road. After braking heavily he claimed that the image seemed to dissolve into the night. This could be an example of an apparition that has been around for a long time. Local folklore tells of the White Lady, or Ladi Wen, often seen in that specific area, and in fact common to South Wales. She was said to direct those who saw her to a hoard of buried treasure placed long ago under one of the ancient Standing Stones nearby. Others tell that she was the lover of a highwayman who was still guarding his spoils buried close by, and this brings us nicely to the next collection of sightings on this country road.

A man was walking from a friend's house in Cefn Cribwr to his own lodgings in Kenfig Hill in the early hours of the morning. The first indication that something was about to happen was a sudden drop of temperature and a feeling that someone or something was following him. Next he heard the distinct sound of a horse neighing that again seemed to come from behind him. Dismissing this as the result of an overactive imagination, he put it down to horses in the adjacent fields that he could not see due to high hedges. However, a few minutes later he heard it again and this time the distinct sound of horses' hooves drifted across the still night air. Later he claimed that these hooves did not sound as though they were on tarmac, but more on a gravel or loose stone. Plucking up the courage he looked behind him, but there was nothing

The B4281 between Aberkenfig and Kenfig.

behind but an empty road. As his journey progressed the sounds appeared to get louder and more frequent, and now what he described as a menacing feeling began to come over him. The next and final escalation of these events was the faint sound of a pistol or gun being discharged, followed by what he described as an inane laugh. Needless to say he needed no prompting to break into a run and was soon back at his lodgings.

Perhaps we can go back to the sixteenth, seventeenth and early eighteenth centuries to look at a possible cause of this and other similar phenomena in this area. Back in these times travellers really did take their lives into their own hands trying to navigate these perilous routes across the open high ground of South Wales. Highwaymen and villains ruled the highways, maps were not available until 1760 and signposts simply did not exist. In our case the ancient row of stone megaliths that probably existed in those days, if followed in bad weather, probably led them off the road and into trouble. The chances of getting lost on these unmade roads, especially during the winter months, or getting held up by a masked horseman was an all too common occurrence and also often fatal. Today we cannot imagine the dangers facing the traveller on this road and it gives a new meaning to the popular term 'Wild West', as it does have the same elements of lawlessness and highway robbery. 'Stand and deliver' is a term we are probably familiar with since childhood; indeed, in those olden times for most travellers their biggest fear was hearing those words when encountering a highwayman. It is believed that the word came into the English language around 1617, although examples of highway robbers date back to medieval and Elizabethan times.

In Welsh folklore the very name 'highwayman' conjures up a romantic image of a bygone age, where men like Twm Sion Cati (Thomas Jones) held up stagecoaches and robbed their rich passengers. The actual origins of the stereotypical highwaymen have their roots in the English Civil War. The execution of Charles I in 1649 left many Royalist officers without a means of support, and as such men had no trade or skill other than soldiering, and they were forced to rob in order to survive. They would often wait around coaching inns and taverns, giving them time to size up their victims and then ride out and wait in a remote place to rob them. Highwaymen had an average life expectancy of under thirty – most died by hanging and then their bodies were hung in gibbets at crossroads as a warning to law breakers. However, it did not deter the local villains and they soon learnt to carry out robbery and murder and blame it on highwaymen. Contemporary accounts suggest that our particular stretch of road, because of its isolation, was a popular haunt of both highwaymen and gangs of robbers. Was this man's encounter with the ghost of a highwayman that perhaps lost his life, or just frequented this stretch of the road? It may also be connected to the White Lady and our next phenomena.

Our last apparition has been seen many times by both locals and people using the road. A former resident of Cefn Cribwr told us this account that happened when she was a young girl in the 1940s. The family lived with their grandparents in the village and it was her grandmother who first alerted her to the subject. She had apparently told her and a younger sister not to look out of their bedroom window that was facing the road if they heard noises or saw lights during the night. She explained that if either of them looked out the fairies could take them away. They told their parents what grandmother had said and their father muttered it was a load of nonsense and told his wife that he would talk to his mother about filling their heads with such rubbish. Of course we all know what happens if you tell a child not to do something, especially as intriguing as this – the elder girl naturally did the opposite.

It was apparently a hot summer's night some months later and she was having trouble sleeping. Suddenly the sound of a trumpet in the distance drifted through the open window. She propped herself on the windowsill and looked out at the road which appeared deserted in both directions. Then coming towards her from the direction of Aberkenfig she could just make out the shape of an old-fashioned carriage drawn by four horses. She remembers that it was travelling faster than any car she had seen on that road up until then and was soon disappearing in the distance. She remembered that at the time she was both excited and scared, although she resolved to keep it to herself in view of her father's comments earlier. It was many years later that she plucked up enough courage to ask her grandmother about the incident. It appears that this was the apparition she had been warned about in her childhood and many had seen or heard it, but there was a conspiracy of silence in the community to avoid ridicule.

There were some aspects of this tale that fit in with known historical facts and the perceived configuration and horn/trumpet sound tends to suggest a stagecoach. It is almost certain that stagecoaches would have used this route. However, it could also have been the carriage of some rich family returning to or visiting Margam, Briton Ferry or even Swansea. Nevertheless, there is one puzzling thing about this and similar apparitions: the speed of the coach. Historic researchers claim that such coaches could only cover 10–12 miles per day and that means a very low average speed, nothing like the alleged speed of such reported apparitions. Even if a highwayman or a gang of robbers were pursuing the ghostly coach, it cannot be a true representation of a real event. It was this woman's original conversation as a child with her long-dead grandmother that perhaps may point in another direction completely. There are some researchers that claim that these speeding coaches are our interpretation of an event from the realms of folklore and mythology.

Some have proposed that this apparition is an interpretation of a legendary event called 'The Wild Hunt'. In olden times, during the furious storms of winter, the country people in this part of Wales would cower in their homes. It is said that in the distance, above the howling wind, could be heard the sound of the pounding of hooves. It was said that if you were foolish enough to glance outside you would see a macabre assortment of men and beasts passing with the speed of the wind. It is often said that the observer was snatched from their home and became part of the hunt for eternity. Another feature of the legendary hunt is headless riders and many reports of such apparitions have been seen accompanying this phantom coach. Whatever the answer, the road between Aberkenfig and Kenfig Hill may just be one of the most haunted in South Wales.

Other local titles published by The History Press

Haunted Cardiff and the Valleys
SOUTH WALES PARANORMAL RESEARCH

Drawing on extensive research and interviews with first-hand witnesses, South Wales Paranormal Research have put together this chilling collection of sightings and mysterious happenings, mostly from the last ten years. Featuring ghostly cars and ships, mysterious policemen and figures in country lanes, this book will appeal to anyone interested in the paranormal or those who wish to read more about tales and legends from Cardiff's shadowy past.

978 0 7524 4378 2

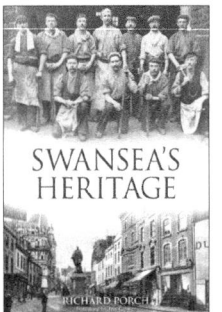

Swansea's Heritage
RICHARD PORCH

In this compilation, Richard Porch brings together a series of people, buildings and events which have created and maintained Swansea's unique character from the Middle Ages to the present day. From the Vikings through Victorian sea captains to Harry and Benjamin Davies, the Upper Bank Coppermen, this compendium also features a geological heritage trail round the city.

Illustrated with old and new photographs, *Swansea's Heritage* will delight anybody interested in the origins of this historic city.

978 0 7524 4559 5

Swansea: History You Can See
RICHARD PORCH

The history of landmarks such as the Lockgate sculpture in Ferrara Quay, the copperworkers' township Hafod and the Whitford Point lighthouse – the only wave-washed cast-iron lighthouse in Britain – is recorded in this A-Z of the people, buildings, industries and events that have shaped the city and county of Swansea. A must-read for residents and newcomers to Swansea alike.

978 0 7524 3076 8

Haunted Bristol
SUE LE' QUEUX

A unique glimpse into the ghostly legacy of Bristol's past that is sure to appeal to anyone interested in a spot of ghost-hunting! This enthralling selection of newspaper reports and first-hand accounts recalls strange and spooky happenings in the city's streets, churches, theatres and public houses. From paranormal manifestations at the Bristol Old Vic to the ghostly activity of a monk who haunts Bristol's twelfth-century cathedral, this spine-tingling collection of supernatural tales is a must-read for those interested in Bristol's haunted heritage.

978 0 7524 3300 4

If you are interested in purchasing other books published by The History Press, or in case you have difficulty finding any History Press books in your local bookshop, you can also place orders directly through our website

www.thehistorypress.co.uk